Calculations in Chemistry

Book 4
Enthalpy Calculations for A-level Chemistry

By T. Everitt

Copyright © T. Everitt

Calculations in Chemistry
A Series of Books for A-Level Students

Chemistry isn't all about calculations. They are not the be-all and end-all of A-level Chemistry either but it helps to be good at them. By definition this isn't a whole course textbook and not one full of exciting new discoveries or colourful content. Nor is it specific to a particular examination board.

The aim of this book is to provide examples to practise on in addition to those in your course textbook, which often do not contain many examples of questions and problems to test your understanding.

Some calculations are relatively simple, others more involved with multiple steps. The aim of this book is to guide you through examples and then give you questions to apply your understanding to. These begin simply but increase in complexity as you progress. Some also drop in the occasional non-calculation parts to keep you grounded in the reality of examination questions. Fully explained answers are included at the back of the book.

There are some key formulae that you **HAVE** to be able to recall. They enable you to answer questions speedily even if the formula is given somewhere in the examination paper and are essential if it is not. This recall also gives you the confidence that you are "doing it right!"

I hope that you find this book useful.

Errors, typographical correction and identified mistakes at **www.mrevbooks.co.uk**

MrEV

Calculations In Chemistry Book Series

Book 1   Moles for A-level Chemistry

Book 2   Concentration and Acid–Alkali Titrations

Book 3   Analysis and Purity Calculations

Book 4   Enthalpy Calculations

Book 5   Entropy and Gibbs Free Energy

Book 6   Acids, Alkalis and Buffers

Book 7   Rate Equations and Equilibria

Book 8   Electrochemical Cells and Redox Equilibria

Enthalpy Calculations

Contents

Part 1 – Experimental Energy Changes

Equation to Learn:

In experimental questions, calculation of the energy exchanged with the surroundings (**Q**) is calculated by the equation below:

$$Q = m\ c\ \Delta T$$

Q = the joules of energy exchanged (usually with a solvent and measured by a thermometer or digital temperature probe).

m = the mass of water heated by the reaction. This is either in a can over a flame for combustion or the mass of water in the combined solutions.

c = the specific heat capacity of water. This is $4.18\ J\ K^{-1}\ g^{-1}$. It is worth remembering this value as it saves time looking it up. It is assumed that solutions have this value as well as water.

ΔT = change in temperature in either K or °C.

The enthalpy change (**ΔH**) is then calculated by:

$$\Delta H = \frac{Q}{moles}$$

The moles should be for the equation as it is written.

Many textbooks now use the format $\Delta_c H^{\ominus}_{298}$ rather than the $\Delta H^{\ominus}_{c\ 298}$ format used in this book. You will see both across a range of sources including Internet sourced documents and texts.

Expected prior knowledge – you are expected to be able to

- Construct correct formulae
- Construct balanced chemical equations
- Rearrange simple mathematical equations
- Calculate formula mass
- Calculate moles of substance from a given mass
- Calculate moles from concentration
- Select appropriate numbers of significant figures for an answer from the data within the question

Example 1

In an experiment using zinc metal to displace a less reactive metal, the following results were collected.

The zinc was the limiting reactant.

Results:

Volume of solution	= 50.0 cm^3
Moles of zinc	= 0.0415 mol
Temperature rise	= 2.70 °C

Calculate the value of ΔH for this reaction using the results above.

Specific heat capacity of water = 4.18 J K^{-1} g^{-1} *[It is worth remembering this value.]*

Q = 50.0 x 4.18 x 2.70 = 564.3 J

ΔH = 564.3 ÷ 0.0415 = 13,597.6 J

ΔH = – 13.6 kJ mol^{-1}

The answer is to 3 s.f due to the data significant figures given in the question.

Example 2

Calculate the value for the enthalpy change of combustion (ΔH$_c^{\ominus}$) from the results.

Calculate the percentage difference to the published value of – 1367 kJ mol^{-1}.

Results:

Volume of water used	= 250.0 cm^3
Mass of ethanol burned	= 0.365 g
Temperature rise	= 7.2 °C
M$_r$[C$_2$H$_5$OH]	= 46.0

Calculate the value of ΔH$_c^{\ominus}$ for this reaction using the results above.

Q = 250.0 x 4.18 x 7.2 = 7,524 J

Moles of ethanol burned = 0.365 ÷ 46.0 = 0.007935 mol

ΔH = 7,524 ÷ 0.007935 = 948,204 J

ΔH$_c^{\ominus}$ = – 950 kJ mol^{-1}

Answer is to 2 s.f due to the accuracy of the temperature rise.

$$\text{Percentage difference} = \frac{Difference}{Published\ value} \ x\ 100\ \%$$

Percentage difference = 100 x (1367 – 950) / 1367 = **30.5 %**

Questions to Test Your Knowledge

Question 1

In the reaction between magnesium metal and zinc chloride the following results were obtained.

Results:

Volume of 0.50 mol dm^{-3} ZnCl$_{2(aq)}$ = 40.0 cm^3

Mass of magnesium   = 0.405 g

Temperature rise   = 1.6 °C

Calculate the value of the enthalpy change (ΔH_R) for this reaction using the results above.

Specific heat capacity of water = 4.18 J K^{-1} g^{-1}

Question 2

Sodium hydrogen carbonate was reacted with HCl$_{(aq)}$ in the equation below.

$$NaHCO_{3(s)} + HCl_{(aq)} \rightarrow NaCl_{(aq)} + CO_{2(g)} + H_2O_{(l)}$$

5.00 g of NaHCO$_{3(s)}$ was reacted with 100.0 cm^3 of 0.25 mol dm^{-3} HCl$_{(aq)}$.

    a)   Calculate whether the NaHCO$_{3(s)}$ or the HCl$_{(aq)}$ is the limiting reactant.

    b)   The temperature dropped by 4.5 °C. Calculate a value for ΔH_R including the correct sign in your answer.

Question 3

50.0 cm^3 of 0.400 mol dm^{-3} K$_2$CO$_{3(aq)}$ was neutralised by 50.0 cm^3 of 0.250 mol dm^{-3} HNO$_{3(aq)}$.

    a)   Calculate whether the K$_2$CO$_3$ or the HNO$_3$ is in excess.

    b)   The temperature rose by 8.4 °C.
            Calculate a value for ΔH_R including a sign in your answer.

Question 4

50.0 cm^3 of 0.250 mol dm^{-3} NaOH$_{(aq)}$ was neutralised by 50.0 cm^3 of 0.250 mol dm^{-3} HNO$_{3(aq)}$.

a) The temperature rose by 1.7 °C. Calculate a value for ΔH_R. Include a sign in your answer.

b) Twice the volume of sodium hydroxide was used with the same volume of nitric acid. State the effect this will have on the temperature rise.

Question 5

The combustion of ethene takes place with a yellow flame in air.

When 480 cm^3 of ethene at RTP was burned through a jet and used to heat 400.0 cm^3 of water, the temperature of the water rose by 10.6 °C.

a) Calculate the value of $\Delta H_c^\ominus$ for ethene from the data above.

1 mole of gas occupies 24.0 dm^3 at room temperature and pressure.

The published value is – 1411 kJ mol^{-1}.

b) Give **TWO** reasons why your answer is less exothermic (smaller in magnitude) than this value.

c) Calculate the percentage difference from the published value.

Question 6

The combustion of 1.160 g of propanone raised the temperature of 455 g of water by 13.3 °C.

a) Calculate the value of $\Delta H_c^\ominus$ for propanone from this experimental data.

M_r [propanone] = 58.0

The published value for the enthalpy of combustion is – 1,816.5 kJ mol^{-1}.

b) Calculate the percentage difference between the experimental value and the published value.

Question 7

Octan-1-ol has the formula $C_8H_{17}OH$ and a formula mass of 130.

The enthalpy of combustion for octan-1-ol is $- 5293.6$ kJ mol^{-1}.

a) Calculate the expected temperature rise when 0.650 g of octan-1-ol is burned beneath a copper can containing 400.0 g of water.

b) Give **TWO** reasons why the actual temperature rise will be smaller than the expected rise in part a).

Part 2 – Enthalpy Cycles

Enthalpy cycles or Hess Cycles are the chemist's version of the concept of "conservation of energy".

One way to view them is like three one-way streets. You either go the correct way down the street or the opposite way to the one-way arrow.

- Go the same way as the arrow… keep the ΔH value with the same sign

- Go the opposite way to the arrow… change the sign, keeping the same numerical value

The two ΔH values are then added together.

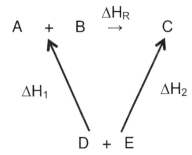

In this cycle, $\Delta H_R = -\Delta H_1 + \Delta H_2$ as the alternative route is the reverse of ΔH_1 but ΔH_2 is used as it is drawn in the cycle.

Expected prior knowledge – you are expected to be able to:

- Construct balanced chemical equations.

- Select appropriate numbers of significant figures for an answer from the data within the question.

- Calculate moles from amounts of mass using A_r and M_r.

- Calculate moles from concentrations and volume as above.

- Know that the enthalpy of formation ($\Delta H_f^\ominus$) of 1 mole of an element in its standard state has a value of zero.

Example 1 – Enthalpy of Formations ($\Delta H_f^{\ominus}$)

Calculate the ΔH_R for the reaction using the ΔH_f values given.

$$C_2H_{4(g)} \quad + \quad HI_{(g)} \quad \rightarrow \quad C_2H_5I_{(l)}$$

Substance	$\Delta H_f^{\ominus}$/ kJ mol^{-1}
$C_2H_{4(g)}$	+ 52.2
$HI_{(g)}$	– 40.7
$C_2H_5I_{(l)}$	+ 26.5

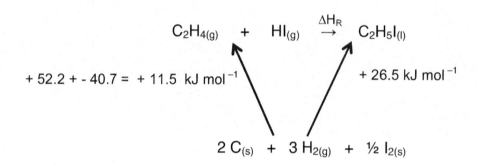

+ 52.2 + - 40.7 = + 11.5 kJ mol^{-1} + 26.5 kJ mol^{-1}

$$\Delta H_R = - (+ 11.5) + (+ 26.5) = - 11.5 + 26.5 = \textbf{+ 15.0 kJ mol}^{-1}$$

Example 2 – Calculating a Missing Value

The reaction to form $TiCl_4$ is shown below.

$$FeTiO_{3(s)} + 7 Cl_{2(g)} + 6 C_{(s)} \rightarrow 2 TiCl_{4(l)} + 2 FeCl_{3(s)} + 6 CO_{(g)}$$

The enthalpy change of the reaction, ΔH_R is $+ 60.8$ kJ mol^{-1}.

Substance	$\Delta H_f^{\ominus}$/ kJ mol^{-1}
$TiCl_{4(l)}$	$- 804.2$
$FeCl_{3(s)}$	$- 399.5$
$CO_{(g)}$	$- 110.5$

[The enthalpy change of formation of any element ($\Delta H_f^{\ominus}$) in its standard state is zero.]

Calculate the value of $\Delta H_f^{\ominus}$ [FeTiO$_3$]

$$2 FeTiO_{3(s)} + 7 Cl_{2(g)} + 6 C_{(s)} \rightarrow 2 TiCl_{4(l)} + 2 FeCl_{3(s)} + 6 CO_{(g)}$$

2x $\Delta H_f^{\ominus}$ [FeTiO$_3$]

2x - 804.2 + 2x – 399.5
= – 2407.4 kJ mol^{-1}

$$Fe_{(s)} + Ti_{(s)} + 7 Cl_{2(g)} + 6 C_{(s)} + 3 O_{2(g)}$$

$\Delta H_R = - 2$ x $\Delta H_f^{\ominus}$ [FeTiO$_3$] $+ - 2407.4 = + 60.8$ kJ mol^{-1}

$- 2$ x $\Delta H_f^{\ominus}$ [FeTiO$_3$] $= - 2407.4 = + 60.8 + 2407.4 = + 2468.2$ kJ mol^{-1}

$\Delta H_f^{\ominus}$ [FeTiO$_3$] $= ½$ x $-2468.2 = - $ **1234.1 kJ mol^{-1}.**

Example 3 – Adding Oxygen for Combustion

Calculate a value for the ΔH_R for the reaction shown below using the enthalpy changes of combustion ($\Delta H_c^{\ominus}$) shown below.

$$\text{butane} \quad \rightarrow \quad \text{2-methylpropane}$$

Substance	$\Delta H_c^{\ominus}$ / kJ mol^{-1}
Butane, C_4H_{10}	-2876.5
2-methylpropane, C_4H_{10}	-2868.5

Add 6.5 O_2 to both sides for the combustion downwards to the CO_2 and H_2O.

This does not affect the ΔH_R value as the oxygen is not reacting in that direction.

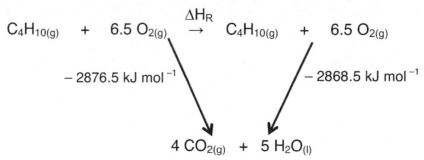

$\Delta H_R = -2876.5 + +2868.5 = $ **$-$8.0 kJ mol^{-1}**

Example 4 – Lattice Energy, Solution and Hydration Cycle

A common Hess Cycle links enthalpy changes for solution, lattice energy and the hydration of ions

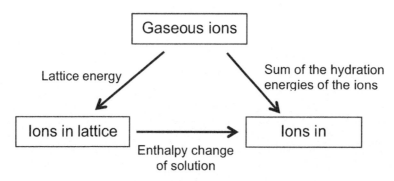

Use the data to calculate the enthalpy change of solution for sodium bromide.

Substance	$\Delta H_{Hydration}$ / kJ mol^{-1}	$\Delta H_{Lattice}$ / kJ mol^{-1}
NaBr		-742
$Na^+_{(g)}$	-405	
$Br^-_{(g)}$	-348	

$\Delta H_{Solution} = -\Delta H_{Lattice} + \Delta H_{Hydration}[Na^+_{(g)}] + \Delta H_{Hydration}[Br^-_{(g)}]$

$\Delta H_{Solution} = +742 - 405 - 348 = $ **$-$11.0 kJ mol^{-1}**

Example 5 – Using Two Experiments to Determine a ΔH Value

These questions involve a reaction that is difficult to determine the value for. An alternative reaction route can be used to create a Hess Cycle that is then used to calculate a value for the impossible reaction.

$KHCO_3$ decomposes at 120 °C to form potassium carbonate.

$$2\ KHCO_{3(s)} \quad \rightarrow \quad K_2CO_{3(s)} \quad + \quad CO_{2(g)} \quad + \quad H_2O_{(l)}$$

The enthalpy change for this reaction is difficult to determine due to the need to heat the potassium hydrogen carbonate in order for it to decompose it and consequently the enthalpy change gets lost within the thermal energy supplied.

Procedure 1

A 1.762 g sample of potassium hydrogen carbonate was reacted with 50.0 cm^3 of dilute $HCl_{(aq)}$, an excess. The temperature fell by 5.50 °C.

Procedure 2

A 2.524 g sample of potassium carbonate was reacted with 50.0 cm^3 of dilute $HCl_{(aq)}$. The temperature rose by 8.40 °C.

Calculate a value for the enthalpy change of decomposition ($ΔH_{dec}$) of 1 mole of potassium hydrogen carbonate.

Procedure 1

Moles of $KHCO_3$ = 1.762 / (39.1 + 1 + 48) = 0.020 moles

Q = 50.0 x 4.18 x 5.5 = +1149.5 J

$ΔH$ = +1149.5 / 0.020 = 57,475 J mol^{-1} = + 57.475 kJ mol^{-1}

Procedure 2

Moles of K_2CO_3 = 2.524 / (2 x 39.1 + 48) = 0.020 moles

Q = 50.0 x 4.18 x 8.4 = – 1755.6 J

$ΔH$ = – 1755.6 / 0.020 = 87,780 J mol^{-1} = – 87.780 kJ mol^{-1}

$$\overset{\Delta H_{dec}}{2\ HCl_{(aq)} \ + \ 2\ KHCO_{3(s)} \ \rightarrow \ K_2CO_{3(s)} \ + \ CO_{2(g)} \ + \ H_2O_{(l)} \ + \ 2\ HCl_{(aq)}}$$

2 x + 57.475 = + 114.95 kJ mol^{-1}
Doubled as 2 $KHCO_3$ in equation

– 87.78 kJ mol^{-1}

$$2\ KCl_{(aq)} \quad + \quad 2\ CO_{2(g)} \quad + \quad 2\ H_2O_{(l)}$$

$ΔH_{dec}$ = + 114.95 – 87.78 = + 27.17 kJ mol^{-1} = **+ 27.2 kJ mol^{-1} to 3 s.f.**

Example 6 – Estimation of ΔH_R Using Bond Energies

Bond energies have limitations. Therefore they only give estimates of a ΔH value for a reaction.

- Bond energies are mean values across a number of compounds
- Bond energies only apply to the gaseous state

Use bond energies to estimate the enthalpy change for the reaction below.

$$CH_3Br_{(g)} \;+\; F_{2(g)} \;\rightarrow\; CH_2FBr_{(g)} \;+\; HF_{(g)}$$

Bond	Energy / kJ mol^{-1}
C – H	+ 435
C – Br	+ 290
F – F	+ 158
H – F	+ 568
C – F	+ 452

Long method

Break	Make
3 x E(C – H) = 3 x 435 = + 1305	2 x E(C – H) = 2 x 435 = – 870
1 x E(C – Br) = 1 x 290 = + 290	1 x E(C – Br) = 1 x 290 = – 290
1 x E(F – F) = 1 x 158 = + 158	1 x E(C – F) = 1 x 158 = – 452
	1 x E(H – F) = 1 x 568 = – 568
Total = + 1753 kJ mol^{-1}	Total = – 2180 kJ mol^{-1}

ΔH_R = +1753 – 2180 = **– 427 kJ mol^{-1}**

Short method – Use only the bonds that change (but be careful, it is easy to miss bonds!)

Break	Make
1 x E(C – H) = 1 x 435 = + 435	1 x E(C – F) = 1 x 158 = – 452
1 x E(F – F) = 1 x 158 = + 158	1 x E(H – F) = 1 x 568 = – 568
Total = + 593 kJ mol^{-1}	Total = – 1020 kJ mol^{-1}

ΔH_R = +593 – 1020 = **– 427 kJ mol^{-1}**

Questions to Test Your Knowledge

Question 8

Calculate the value for ΔH_R for the reaction below.

$$CH_{4(g)} + H_2O_{(g)} \rightarrow CO_{(g)} + 3 H_{2(g)}$$

Substance	$\Delta H_f^{\ominus}$ / kJ mol^{-1}
$CH_{4(g)}$	− 74.8
Steam, $H_2O_{(g)}$	− 241.8
$CO_{(g)}$	− 110.5

Question 9

Calculate a value for ΔH_R for the reaction below.

$$2 Sr(NO_3)_2.4H_2O_{(s)} \rightarrow 2 SrO_{(s)} + 4 NO_{2(g)} + O_{2(g)} + 8 H_2O_{(g)}$$

Substance	$\Delta H_f^{\ominus}$ / kJ mol^{-1}
$Sr(NO_3)_2.4H_2O_{(s)}$	− 2154.8
Steam, $H_2O_{(g)}$	− 241.8
$SrO_{(s)}$	− 592.0
$NO_{2(g)}$	+ 33.2

Question 10

Calculate a value for ΔH_R for the reaction below.

$$Al_2Se_{3(s)} + 3 H_2O_{(l)} \rightarrow Al_2O_{3(s)} + 3 H_2Se_{(g)}$$

Substance	$\Delta H_f^{\ominus}$ / kJ mol^{-1}
$Al_2Se_{3(s)}$	− 566.9
Liquid water, $H_2O_{(l)}$	− 285.8
$Al_2O_{3(s)}$	− 1675.7
H_2Se	+ 29.7

Question 11

Calculate a value for $\Delta H_f^{\ominus}$ of carbon disulfide, $CS_{2(l)}$ using the data and reaction below.

$$CS_{2(l)} + 3\,O_{2(g)} \rightarrow CO_{2(g)} + 2\,SO_{2(g)} \qquad \Delta H_R = -\,1076.8 \text{ kJ mol}^{-1}$$

Substance	$\Delta H_f^{\ominus}$ / kJ mol^{-1}
$CO_{2(g)}$	$-$ 393.5
$SO_{2(g)}$	$-$ 296.8

Question 12

Calculate a value for $\Delta H_f^{\ominus}$ thallium carbonate, Tl_2CO_3 from the data and reaction below.

$$2\,TlOH_{(s)} + CO_{2(g)} \rightarrow Tl_2CO_{3(s)} + H_2O_{(l)} \qquad \Delta H_R = -\,488.1 \text{ kJ mol}^{-1}$$

Substance	$\Delta H_f^{\ominus}$ / kJ mol^{-1}
$TlOH_{(s)}$	$-$ 104.2
Liquid water, $H_2O_{(l)}$	$-$ 285.8
$CO_{2(g)}$	$-$ 393.5
$Tl_2CO_{3(s)}$	$-$ 700.0

Question 13

Estimate the enthalpy change for the addition of chlorine to propene using the bond energy data shown below.

$$C_3H_{6(g)} + Cl_{2(g)} \rightarrow C_3H_6Cl_{2(s)}$$

Bond	Energy / kJ mol^{-1}
C $-$ H	+ 413
C $-$ Cl	+ 346
Cl $-$ Cl	+ 243
C $-$ C	+ 347
C $=$ C	+ 612

Question 14

a)   Estimate the value of the enthalpy change for the combustion of ethanedioic acid in an excess of oxygen.

$$C_2H_2O_{4(s)} \ + \ ½ \, O_{2(g)} \ \rightarrow \ 2 \, CO_{2(g)} \ + \ H_2O_{(l)}$$

Bond	Energy / kJ mol^{-1}
C – C	+ 347
O – H	+ 464
C – O	+ 358
C = O	+ 805
O = O	+ 498

Ethanedioic acid

The published value is – 243.3 kJ mol^{-1}.

b)   Explain the difference between your answer to part a) and this value.

Question 15

Sulfur tetrafluoride reacts with steam in the reaction below.

$$SF_{4(g)} \ + \ 2 \, H_2O_{(g)} \ \rightarrow \ SO_{2(g)} \ + \ 4 \, HF_{(g)}$$

Bond	Energy / kJ mol^{-1}
H – O	+ 464
S = O	+ 523
H – F	+ 568

Substance	$\Delta H_f^{\ominus}$ / kJ mol^{-1}
$H_2O_{(g)}$	– 241.8
$SF_{4(g)}$	– 774.9
$SO_{2(g)}$	– 296.8
$HF_{(g)}$	– 271.1

a)   Calculate the enthalpy change for the reaction using the $\Delta H_f^{\ominus}$ values.

b)   Use your answer to part a) and the bond energy data above to estimate the bond energy of the S – F bond in kJ mol^{-1}. Give your answer as a whole number.

Question 16

Calculate the value of $\Delta H_c^{\ominus}[C_3H_6O_{(l)}]$.

$$3\ C_{(s)} \quad + \quad 3\ H_{2(g)} \quad + \quad \tfrac{1}{2}\ O_{2(g)} \quad \rightarrow \quad C_3H_6O_{(l)}$$

$\Delta H_f^{\ominus}[C_3H_6O_{(l)}] \quad = -\ 248.0\ kJ\ mol^{-1}$

$\Delta H_c^{\ominus}[C_{(s,\ graphite)}] = -\ 393.5\ kJ\ mol^{-1}$

$\Delta H_c^{\ominus}[H_{2(g)}] \quad\quad = -\ 285.8\ kJ\ mol^{-1}$

Question 17

a)   Use the data below to calculate the enthalpy change of solution for $SrI_{2(s)}$.

$\Delta H_{Lattice}[SrI_{2(s)}] \quad = -\ 1963\ kJ\ mol^{-1}$

$\Delta H_{Hyd}[Sr^{2+}_{(g)}] \quad = -\ 1446\ kJ\ mol^{-1}$

$\Delta H_{Hyd}[I^-_{(g)}] \quad\quad = -\ 308\ kJ\ mol^{-1}$

b)   Use the data below to calculate the enthalpy of hydration for a bromide ion.

$\Delta H_{Lattice}[MgBr_{2(s)}] \quad = -\ 2440\ kJ\ mol^{-1}$

$\Delta H_{Hyd}[Mg^{2+}_{(g)}] \quad = -\ 1926\ kJ\ mol^{-1}$

$\Delta H_{Sol}[MgBr_{2(s)}] \quad = -\ 182\ kJ\ mol^{-1}$

Question 18

Calculate the value of $\Delta H_f^{\ominus}[C_6H_{6(l)}]$.

$$6\ C_{(s)} \quad + \quad 3\ H_{2(g)} \quad \rightarrow \quad C_6H_{6(l)}$$

$\Delta H_c^{\ominus}[C_6H_{6(l)}] \quad = -\ 3267.4\ kJ\ mol^{-1}$

$\Delta H_c^{\ominus}[C_{(s,\ graphite)}] = -\ 393.5\ kJ\ mol^{-1}$

$\Delta H_c^{\ominus}[H_{2(g)}] \quad\quad = -\ 285.8\ kJ\ mol^{-1}$

Question 19

a)   Calculate the enthalpy change of solution for the four potassium halides.

$\Delta H_{Lattice}[KF_{(s)}]$	$= -\ 817\ kJ\ mol^{-1}$	$\Delta H_{Hyd}[F^-_{(g)}]$	$= -\ 524\ kJ\ mol^{-1}$
$\Delta H_{Lattice}[KCl_{(s)}]$	$= -\ 711\ kJ\ mol^{-1}$	$\Delta H_{Hyd}[Cl^-_{(g)}]$	$= -\ 378\ kJ\ mol^{-1}$
$\Delta H_{Lattice}[KBr_{(s)}]$	$= -\ 679\ kJ\ mol^{-1}$	$\Delta H_{Hyd}[Br^-_{(g)}]$	$= -\ 348\ kJ\ mol^{-1}$
$\Delta H_{Lattice}[KI_{(s)}]$	$= -\ 651\ kJ\ mol^{-1}$	$\Delta H_{Hyd}[I^-_{(g)}]$	$= -\ 308\ kJ\ mol^{-1}$
$\Delta H_{Hyd}[K^+_{(g)}]$	$= -\ 320\ kJ\ mol^{-1}$		

b)   State whether the temperature would rise or fall when each is dissolved.

Question 20

Barium carbonate will decompose if heated very strongly. However, this does make it impossible to determine the value of the enthalpy change for the reaction.

Two experiments were carried out to determine the values of ΔH_1 and ΔH_2 in the Hess Cycle shown below.

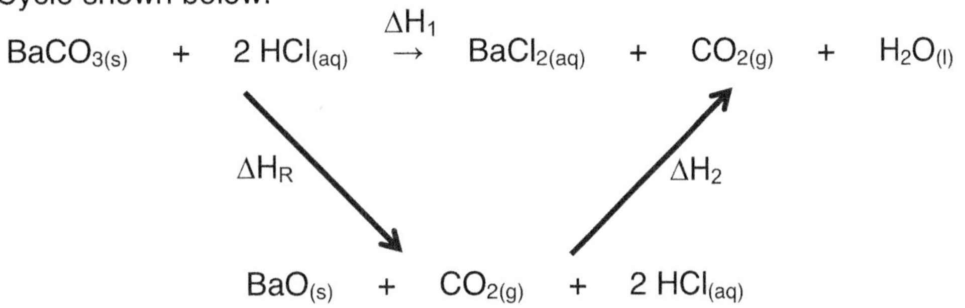

$$BaCO_{3(s)} \quad + \quad 2\,HCl_{(aq)} \quad \xrightarrow{\Delta H_1} \quad BaCl_{2(aq)} \quad + \quad CO_{2(g)} \quad + \quad H_2O_{(l)}$$

$\Delta H_R \searrow \qquad\qquad\qquad \nearrow \Delta H_2$

$$BaO_{(s)} \quad + \quad CO_{2(g)} \quad + \quad 2\,HCl_{(aq)}$$

Experiment 1:

A 7.89 g sample of $BaCO_{3(s)}$ was reacted with 50.0 cm^3 of 2.00 mol dm^{-3} $HCl_{(aq)}$. The temperature of the solution rose by 9.65 °C.

Experiment 2:

A 10.73 g sample of $BaO_{(s)}$ was reacted with 400.0 cm^3 of 0.500 mol dm^{-3} $HCl_{(aq)}$. The temperature of the solution rose by 12.55 °C.

a)   Calculate the enthalpy change corresponding to ΔH_1.

b)   Calculate the enthalpy change corresponding to ΔH_2.

c)   Combine your answers to parts a) and b) to find the value of ΔH_R.

Part 3 – Born-Haber Cycles

Born-Haber Cycles are specific Hess Cycles that involve Lattice Energy.

In some textbooks lattice energies are exothermic (from gaseous ions to solid) while in other texts they are endothermic and involve the separation of the ions in a lattice (solid to gaseous ions). In either case, the answer is numerically identical, just with the opposite sign.

In this book, lattice energies are assumed to be negative values and therefore exothermic.

Born-Haber Cycles involve a number of constituent enthalpy changes.

You need to know these definitions.

Expected prior knowledge – you are expected to be able to:

- Construct a Hess Cycle

- Select appropriate numbers of significant figures for an answer from the data within the question.

- Define enthalpy change of formation, $\Delta H_f^{\ominus}$ and know it is zero for element formation in their standard states.

- Know that the enthalpy change of atomisation, $\Delta H_{at}^{\ominus}$, is the formation of one mole of separate atoms from the element in its standard state. (For diatomic gases it is therefore from ½ mole of X_2.)

- Know that ionisation energy is the formation of ions in the gaseous state and that it is an endothermic process with the symbol E_{mx} where x is the electron number being removed.

- Know that electron affinity is the addition of an electron to gaseous atoms or ions with the symbol ΔH_{aff}.

Note: Some texts use variations on these symbols.

Example 1 – Calculating a Lattice Energy

Calculate the value of the lattice energy for magnesium chloride using the data below.

Enthalpy change	Value / kJ mol^{-1}
$\Delta H_{at}^{\ominus} [Mg_{(s)}]$	+ 147.7
$\Delta H_{at}^{\ominus} [\frac{1}{2} Cl_{2(g)}]$	+ 121.7
1st ionisation energy of $Mg_{(g)}$, E_{m1}	+ 738.0
2nd ionisation energy of $Mg_{(g)}$, E_{m2}	+ 1451
Electron affinity, $\Delta H_{aff} [Cl_{(g)}]$	− 348.8
$\Delta H_{f}^{\ominus} [MgCl_{2(s)}]$	− 641.3

These values are laid out in a Born-Haber Cycle.
(You may find some variation on layout in textbooks and in your notes.)

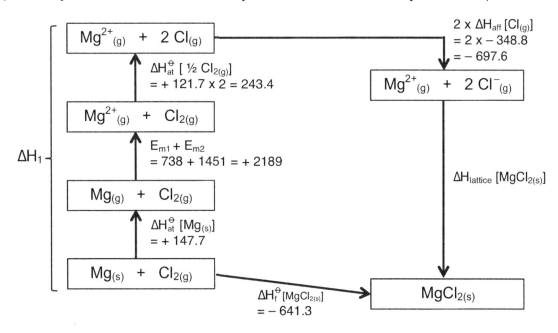

It is often more reliable to combine all the enthalpy changes that convert the elements into the gaseous ions and call this ΔH_1.

$\Delta H_1 = +147.7 + 2189 + 243.4 + - 697.6 = + 1882.5$ kJ mol^{-1}

$\Delta H_{lattice} = - \Delta H_1 + \Delta H_f^{\ominus} [MgCl_{2(s)}] = - 1882.5 - 641.3 = - 2523.8$ kJ mol^{-1}

$\Delta H_{lattice} = - 2524$ kJ mol^{-1} to 4 s.f.

Example 2 – Calculating a Missing Value

Calculate the value of the electron affinity of the F atom using the data below.

Enthalpy change	Value / kJ mol^{-1}
$\Delta H_{at}^{\ominus} \, [Al_{(s)}]$	+ 326.4
$\Delta H_{at}^{\ominus} \, [\, \tfrac{1}{2} \, F_{2(g)}]$	+ 79.0
1st ionisation energy of $Al_{(g)}$, E_{m1}	+ 578.0
2nd ionisation energy of $Al_{(g)}$, E_{m2}	+ 1817
3rd ionisation energy of $Al_{(g)}$, E_{m3}	+ 2745
$\Delta H_{f}^{\ominus} [AlF_{3(s)}]$	− 1504.1
$\Delta H_{lattice} \, [AlF_{3(s)}]$	− 6224

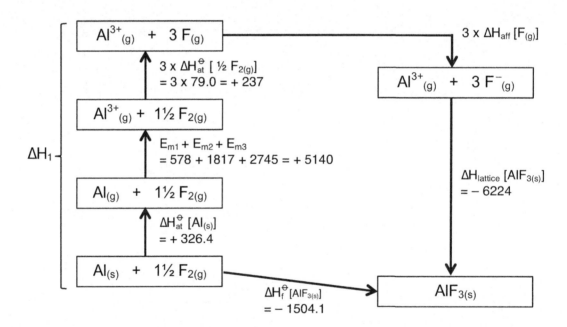

$\Delta H_1 = 326.4 + 5140 + 237 + 3 \times \Delta H_{aff} \, [F_{(g)}] = + 5703.4 + 3 \times \Delta H_{aff} \, [F_{(g)}]$

$3 \times \Delta H_{aff} \, [F_{(g)}] = − 5703.4 − 1504.1 + 6224 = − 983.5$

$\Delta H_{aff} \, [F_{(g)}] = 983.5 \div 3 = − \textbf{327.8 kJ mol}^{-1}$

Questions to Test Your Knowledge

Question 21

Calculate the lattice energy of potassium bromide from the data below.

Enthalpy change	Value / kJ mol^{-1}
$\Delta H^{\ominus}_{at}$ [K$_{(s)}$]	+ 89.2
$\Delta H^{\ominus}_{at}$ [½ Br$_{2(g)}$]	+ 111.9
1st ionisation energy of K$_{(g)}$, E$_{m1}$	+ 419
$\Delta H^{\ominus}_{f}$ [KBr$_{(s)}$]	− 393.8
ΔH_{aff} [Br$_{(g)}$]	− 324.6

Question 22

Calculate the lattice energy of lithium oxide from the data below.

Enthalpy change	Value / kJ mol^{-1}
$\Delta H^{\ominus}_{at}$ [Li$_{(s)}$]	+ 159.4
$\Delta H^{\ominus}_{at}$ [½ O$_{2(g)}$]	+ 249.2
1st ionisation energy of Li$_{(g)}$, E$_{m1}$	+ 520
$\Delta H^{\ominus}_{f}$ [Li$_2$O$_{(s)}$]	− 597.9
ΔH_{aff} [O$_{(g)}$]	− 141.1
ΔH_{aff} [O$^-_{(g)}$]	+ 798

Question 23

Calculate the lattice energy of calcium iodide from the data below.

Enthalpy change	Value / kJ mol^{-1}
$\Delta H^{\ominus}_{at}$ [Ca$_{(s)}$]	+ 178.2
$\Delta H^{\ominus}_{at}$ [½ I$_{2(g)}$]	+ 106.8
1st ionisation energy of Ca$_{(g)}$, E$_{m1}$	+ 590
2nd ionisation energy of Ca$_{(g)}$, E$_{m2}$	+ 1145
$\Delta H^{\ominus}_{f}$ [CaI$_{2(s)}$]	− 533.5
ΔH_{aff} [I$_{(g)}$]	− 295.4

Question 24

Calculate the lattice energy of aluminium oxide from the data below.

Enthalpy change	Value / kJ mol^{-1}
$\Delta H_{at}^{\ominus}$ [Al$_{(s)}$]	+ 326.4
$\Delta H_{at}^{\ominus}$ [½ O$_{2(g)}$]	+ 249.2
1st ionisation energy of Al$_{(g)}$, E$_{m1}$	+ 578
2nd ionisation energy of Al$_{(g)}$, E$_{m2}$	+ 1817
3rd ionisation energy of Al$_{(g)}$, E$_{m3}$	+ 2745
$\Delta H_f^{\ominus}$[Al$_2$O$_{3(s)}$]	− 1675.7
ΔH_{aff} [O$_{(g)}$]	− 141.1
ΔH_{aff} [O$^-_{(g)}$]	+ 798

Question 25

Calculate a value for the enthalpy change of atomisation of gallium from the data below for gallium chloride.

Enthalpy change	Value / kJ mol^{-1}
$\Delta H_{at}^{\ominus}$ [½ Cl$_{2(g)}$]	+ 121.7
1st ionisation energy of Ga$_{(g)}$, E$_{m1}$	+ 579
2nd ionisation energy of Ga$_{(g)}$, E$_{m2}$	+ 1979
3rd ionisation energy of Ga$_{(g)}$, E$_{m3}$	+ 2963
$\Delta H_f^{\ominus}$[GaCl$_{3(s)}$]	− 524.7
ΔH_{aff} [Cl$_{(g)}$]	− 348.8
$\Delta H_{lattice}$ [GaCl$_{3(s)}$]	− 5641

Question 26

Calculate a value for the electron affinity of the S^- ion from the data below for magnesium sulfide.

Enthalpy change	Value / kJ mol^{-1}
$\Delta H_{at}^{\ominus}$ [Mg$_{(s)}$]	+ 147.7
$\Delta H_{at}^{\ominus}$ [S$_{(g)}$]	+ 278.8
1st ionisation energy of Mg$_{(g)}$, E$_{m1}$	+ 738
2nd ionisation energy of Mg$_{(g)}$, E$_{m2}$	+ 1451
$\Delta H_{f}^{\ominus}$ [MgS$_{(s)}$]	− 346.0
ΔH_{aff} [S$_{(g)}$]	− 200.4
$\Delta H_{lattice}$ [MgS$_{(s)}$]	− 3401

Question 27

Calculate the enthalpy change of formation of aluminium selenide from the data below.

Enthalpy change	Value / kJ mol^{-1}
$\Delta H_{at}^{\ominus}$ [Al$_{(s)}$]	+ 326.4
$\Delta H_{at}^{\ominus}$ [Se$_{(s)}$]	+ 227.1
1st ionisation energy of Al$_{(g)}$, E$_{m1}$	+ 578
2nd ionisation energy of Al$_{(g)}$, E$_{m2}$	+ 1817
3rd ionisation energy of Al$_{(g)}$, E$_{m3}$	+ 2745
$\Delta H_{lattice}$ [Al$_2$Se$_{3(s)}$]	− 12,499
ΔH_{aff} [Se$_{(g)}$]	− 195.0
ΔH_{aff} [Se$^-{}_{(g)}$]	+ 301

Examination Style Questions

Question 1

The combustion of 0.0100 moles of a hydrocarbon raises the temperature of 500.0 g of water by 26.2 °C.

a) Calculate the $\Delta H_c^{\ominus}$ of the hydrocarbon. Include a sign in your answer.   (3)

Specific heat capacity of water = 4.18 J K^{-1} g^{-1}

$\Delta H_c^{\ominus}$ to 3 s.f = ... kJ mol^{-1}

b) Give **TWO** major reasons why the magnitude of your answer will be less than the published value.   (2)

Reason 1: ....

....

....

Reason 2: ....

....

....

Total = 5 marks

Question 2

Substance M is soluble in water. It has the formula MF_2.

Dissolving 0.0550 moles of **substance M** in 255.0 g of water causes the temperature of the water to fall by 0.86 °C.

a) Calculate the $\Delta H^{\ominus}_{solution}$ of **substance M**. Give your answer to an appropriate number of significant figures.   (3)

   Specific heat capacity of water = 4.18 J K^{-1} g^{-1}

$\Delta H^{\ominus}_{solution}$ = ... kJ mol^{-1}

b) Complete the Hess Cycle below by filling in the missing information and species.   (2)

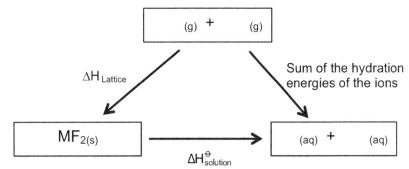

Substance	$\Delta H_{Hydration}$ / kJ mol^{-1}	$\Delta H_{Lattice}$ / kJ mol^{-1}
$MF_{2(s)}$		− 1755
$F^-_{(g)}$	− 524	

c) Use your answer to part a) and the data on the previous page to calculate the hydration energy of the ion of the **metal M**.

Give your answer to an appropriate number of significant figures. (3)

$\Delta H^{\ominus}_{hydration}$ = ... kJ mol^{-1}

Total = 8 marks

Question 3

Strontium carbonate decomposes to release $CO_{2(g)}$ when strongly heated.

$$SrCO_{3(s)} \xrightarrow{\Delta H_R} SrO_{(s)} + CO_{2(g)}$$

Substance	$\Delta H_f^{\ominus}$ / kJ mol^{-1}
$SrCO_{3(s)}$	-1220.1
$SrO_{(s)}$	-592.0
$CO_{2(g)}$	-393.5

a) Use the data in the table above to complete the Hess Cycle below. Use the cycle to calculate ΔH_R for the thermal decomposition of $SrCO_{3(s)}$. Give your answer to an appropriate number of significant figures. (3)

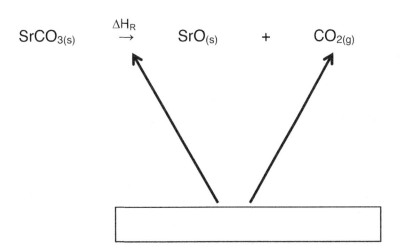

$$\Delta H_R = \text{.......................................} \text{ kJ mol}^{-1}$$

b) Give a reason why $SrCO_3$ needs to be heated for it to decompose. (1)

....

....

c) State why it is difficult to measure the ΔH_R of thermal decomposition reactions directly. (1)

....

....

....

....

Total = 5 marks

Question 4

Methane will react with bromine in the presence of ultraviolet light.

One of the reactions taking place is shown below.

$$CH_{4(g)} + Br_{2(g)} \rightarrow CH_3Br_{(g)} + HBr_{(g)}$$

Bond	Energy / kJ mol^{-1}
C – H	+ 435
Br – Br	+ 193
C – Br	+ 290
H – Br	+ 366

a)   What colour change would you observe as the reaction took place.   (1)

    ....

b)   Use the bond energies above to estimate the enthalpy change of this
      reaction.   (3)

                    ΔH_R = ... kJ mol^{-1}

c)   What is the name of the mechanism of this type of reaction?   (1)

    ....

d)   What is the role of the ultraviolet light?   (1)

    ....

    ....

    ....

                                                              Total = 6 marks

Question 5

Magnesium iodide is an ionic substance with the formula $MgI_{2(s)}$.

Enthalpy change	Value / kJ mol^{-1}
$\Delta H^{\ominus}_{at} [Mg_{(s)}]$	+ 147.7
$\Delta H^{\ominus}_{at} [½ I_{2(g)}]$	+ 106.8
1st ionisation energy of $Mg_{(g)}$, E_{m1}	+ 738
2nd ionisation energy of $Mg_{(g)}$, E_{m2}	+ 1451
$\Delta H^{\ominus}_{f} [MgI_{2(s)}]$	− 364.0
$\Delta H_{aff} [I_{(g)}]$	− 295.4

a) Write the equation for the second ionisation energy of magnesium.
Include state symbols in your answer. (1)

    ....

b) Give a reason why the second ionisation energy of Mg is higher than its
first ionisation energy. (1)

    Reason: ....

    ....

c) Complete the **THREE** missing parts of the Born-Haber Cycle below for
$MgI_{2(s)}$ in the empty boxes. Numerical values are **not** required. (3)

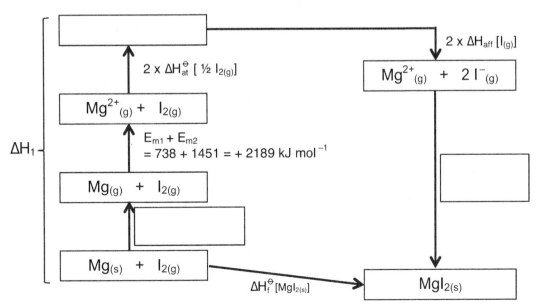

d)   Calculate the lattice energy of magnesium iodide.   (3)

$\Delta H_{Lattice}$ = ... kJ mol^{-1}

The theoretical value for the lattice energy based upon the attraction of spherical charges is – 1944 kJ mol^{-1}.

e)   (i)   Calculate the percentage difference between your answer in part d) and this value.   (2)

      (ii)   Give an explanation for the percentage difference you have calculated in part e) (i).   (3)

....

....

....

....

....

....

....

Total = 13 marks

Question 6

Neutralisation reactions between acids and alkalis are exothermic reactions.

Three reactions were carried out and the results are shown below.

Expt	Acid	Alkali	Temperature rise / K
1	100.0 cm^3 of 1.00 mol dm^{-3} HCl$_{(aq)}$	100.0 cm^3 of 1.00 mol dm^{-3} NaOH$_{(aq)}$	6.9
2	40.0 cm^3 of 2.00 mol dm^{-3} HNO$_{3(aq)}$	40.0 cm^3 of 2.00 mol dm^{-3} KOH$_{(aq)}$	13.9
3	20.0 cm^3 of 2.00 mol dm^{-3} H$_2$SO$_{4(aq)}$	40.0 cm^3 of 2.00 mol dm^{-3} NaOH$_{(aq)}$	18.4

a)   Show for **Expt 3** that neither reagent is in excess.   (2)

b)   Calculate $\Delta H^{\ominus}_{neut}$ per mole of acid for each of the three experiments giving the correct sign and units.   (6)

Expt 1	Expt 2	Expt 3
$\Delta H^{\ominus}_{neut}$ =	$\Delta H^{\ominus}_{neut}$ =	$\Delta H^{\ominus}_{neut}$ =

c) Comment on the values of $\Delta H^{\ominus}_{neut}$ in each of the three experiments. (2)

....

....

....

....

....

Total = 10 marks

Question 7

The following experiment was carried out to determine the enthalpy change for the reaction between silver ions and copper metal.

1. 200.0 cm^3 of 0.100 mol dm^{-3} solution of silver nitrate was placed in a polystyrene cup calorimeter with a lid.
2. The temperature of the solution was measured then 1.00 g of copper powder was added.
3. The solution was gently stirred and the maximum temperature noted.

a) Write a balanced ionic equation for the reaction including state symbols. (2)

....

b) Show by calculation that the copper is in excess. (2)

c) Calculate ΔH_R per mole of copper atoms giving your answer to an appropriate number of significant figures, including a sign and units.
Temperature rise = 0.26 °C (2)

Specific heat capacity of water = 4.18 J K^{-1} g^{-1}

ΔH_R = ...

d) How could you change the procedure to reduce the uncertainty in the temperature change without changing the apparatus used? (1)

....

....

....

....

Total = 7 marks

Question 8

Due to the heat that needs to be supplied it is difficult to determine the enthalpy of decomposition of calcium carbonate.

To find the value of this enthalpy change, two experiments were carried out using pieces of calcite (calcium carbonate) so that a value for $\Delta H_{dec}[CaCO_3]$ could be calculated from experimental data.

Procedure 1

A piece of calcite of mass 2.50 g was heated strongly for 15 minutes to fully decompose the $CaCO_3$ into $CaO_{(s)}$.
The resulting CaO was added to 20.0 cm^3 of dilute $HCl_{(aq)}$ (an excess).
The acid reacted with the CaO and the temperature rose by 24.5 °C.

Procedure 2

A piece of calcite of mass 2.75 g was added to 20.0 cm^3 of dilute $HCl_{(aq)}$ (an excess).
The temperature rose by 4.50 °C.

Specific heat capacity of water = 4.18 J K^{-1} g^{-1}

a)   State whether the decomposition of calcite is likely to be exothermic or endothermic.   (1)

    ....

b)   Write the balanced equation for the reaction of $CaO_{(s)}$ with $HCl_{(aq)}$. Include state symbols in your answer.   (2)

    ....

c)   Calculate the enthalpy change (ΔH_{R1}) for **Procedure 1**.   (3)

ΔH_{R1} = ... kJ mol^{-1}

d)   Write the balanced equation for the reaction of $CaCO_{3(s)}$ with $HCl_{(aq)}$. Include state symbols in your answer.   (2)

    ....

e)   Calculate the enthalpy change (ΔH_{R2}) for **Procedure 2**.   (3)

$$\Delta H_{R2} = \text{...................................... kJ mol}^{-1}$$

f)   Complete the Hess Cycle using ΔH_{dec}, ΔH_{R1} and ΔH_{R2} and fill in the correct products.   (3)

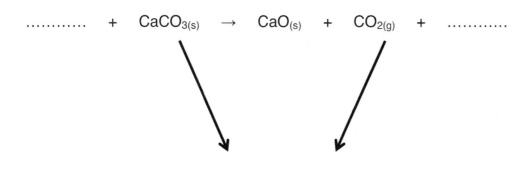

....   + $CaCO_{3(s)}$ $\rightarrow$ $CaO_{(s)}$ + $CO_{2(g)}$ + ...

....

g)   Use the Hess Cycle in part f) to calculate a value for $\Delta H_{dec}[CaCO_3]$. Give your answer to an appropriate number of significant figures.   (2)

$$\Delta H_{dec} = \text{...................................... kJ mol}^{-1}$$

Total = 16 marks

Question 9

The hydrocarbon C_3H_6 will combust in an excess of oxygen with the complete combustion equation below.

$$C_3H_{6(g)} \quad + \quad 4.5 \ O_{2(g)} \quad \rightarrow \quad 3 \ CO_{2(g)} \quad + \quad 3 \ H_2O_{(g)}$$

The formula C_3H_6 has two isomers, propene and cyclopropane.

Bond	Energy / kJ mol^{-1}
C – H	+ 413
C – C	+ 347
C = C	+ 612
O = O	+ 498
O – H	+ 464
C = O	+ 805

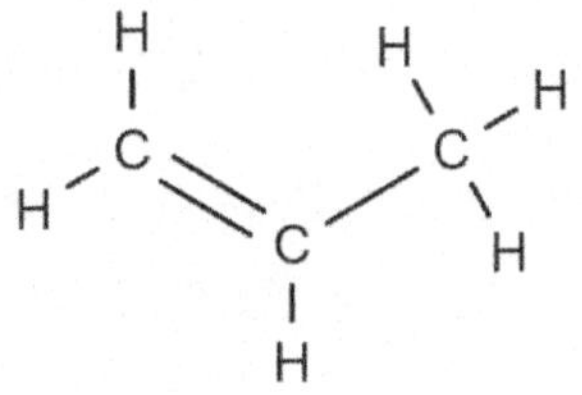

Propene

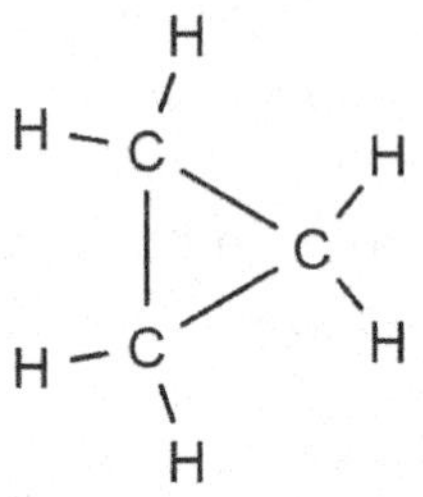

Cyclopropane

a)   Calculate the enthalpy change of combustion ($\Delta H_c^\ominus$) for both isomers using the bond energies above.
Include units and give your answer to an appropriate number of significant figures.   (6)

Propene	Cyclopropane
$\Delta H_c^\ominus$ [propene] =	$\Delta H_c^\ominus$ [cyclopropane] =

b)   Explain why the two values for $\Delta H_c^\ominus$ are not the same despite forming the same products.   (2)

....

....

....

....

....

....

Total = 8 marks

Question 10

Magnesium carbonate can be precipitated by the addition of $Na_2CO_{3(aq)}$ to a solution of magnesium nitrate $(Mg(NO_3)_{2(aq)})$.

The precipitation was carried out twice using the following quantities.

Expt.	Concentration of $Mg(NO_3)_{2(aq)}$	Volume used / cm^3	Concentration of $Na_2CO_{3(aq)}$	Volume used / cm^3	Initial temperature /°C	Final temperature /°C	ΔT / K
1	1.0 mol dm^{-3}	20.0	1.0 mol dm^{-3}	20.0	21.2	24.2	
2	0.20 mol dm^{-3}	50.0	0.20 mol dm^{-3}	50.0	n/a	n/a	

a) Calculate the temperature change for **Expt 1**. Insert your answer into the table with an appropriate number of significant figures. (1)

b) Calculate the expected temperature change for **Expt. 2**. Insert your answer into the table with an appropriate number of decimal places. (3)

c) Which piece of equipment would give a more accurate measurement of the temperatures than a thermometer? (1)

....

d) Write the ionic equation for the precipitation of magnesium carbonate. Include state symbols in your answer. (2)

....

e) Calculate the enthalpy change of the precipitation reaction (ΔH_{pptn}) using the results of **Expt. 1**.
Give your answer to an appropriate number of significant figures. (3)

Specific heat capacity of water = 4.18 J K^{-1} g^{-1}

ΔH_{pptn} = ... kJ mol^{-1}

Total = 10 marks

Question 11

One of the stages in the production of strontium metal involves the reaction of strontium sulfate with carbon at high temperature as shown in the reaction below.

$$SrSO_{4(s)} \quad + \quad 4\,C_{(s)} \quad \rightarrow \quad SrS_{(s)} \quad + \quad 4\,CO_{(g)}$$

Substance	$\Delta H_f^{\ominus}$ / kJ mol^{-1}
$SrSO_{4(s)}$	− 1453.1
$SrS_{(s)}$	− 453.1
$CO_{(g)}$	− 110.5

a) Suggest **ONE** essential safety precaution when carrying out this reaction in the laboratory apart from safety goggles. Give a reason for your answer.

(2)

....

....

....

b) Suggest why it is impossible to measure the enthalpy change for this reaction directly

(1)

....

....

....

c) State why the value for the standard enthalpy change of formation of carbon is zero?

(1)

....

....

d) Use the data above to determine the enthalpy change for this reaction. (2)

ΔH_R = ... kJ mol^{-1}

Total = 6 marks

Question 12

But-1-ene is a flammable gaseous hydrocarbon with the formula $C_4H_{8(g)}$.

a) Write the balanced equation for the combustion in an excess of oxygen. Include state symbols in your answer.   (2)

....

Substance	$\Delta H_c^\ominus$ / kJ mol^{-1}	$\Delta H_f^\ominus$ / kJ mol^{-1}
$C_4H_{8(g)}$	-2716.8	
$CO_{2(g)}$	n/a	-393.5
$H_2O_{(l)}$	n/a	-285.8

Table 1

b) Complete the Hess Cycle and use the data above to calculate a value for $\Delta H_f^\ominus[C_4H_{8(g)}]$.   (5)

$$\Delta H_f^\ominus[C_4H_{8(g)}]$$
$$\ldots\ldots\ldots \quad + \quad 4\ C_{(s)} \quad + \quad 4\ H_{2(g)} \quad \rightarrow \quad C_4H_{8(g)} \quad + \quad \ldots\ldots\ldots$$

$\Delta H_f^\ominus$ = ...kJ mol^{-1}

c) Use your equation from part a) and the bond energies below to estimate a value for the enthalpy change of combustion of but-1-ene. (3)

Bond	Energy / kJ mol^{-1}
C – H	+ 413
C – C	+ 347
C = C	+ 612
O = O	+ 498
O – H	+ 464
C = O	+ 805

$\Delta H_c^{\ominus}$ = ... kJ mol^{-1}

d) Explain why your answer to part c) and the value of $\Delta H_c^{\ominus}$ [but-1-ene] in **Table 1** at the start of the question differ. (2)

....

....

....

....

....

....

....

....

Total = 12 marks

Question 13

Arsenic reacts with fluorine gas according to the balanced equation below.

$$2\ As_{(s)} \quad + \quad 3\ F_{2(g)} \quad \rightarrow \quad 2\ AsF_{3(g)} \qquad \Delta H_R = -\ 1841.2\ kJ\ mol^{-1}$$

Substance	$\Delta H_{at}^{\ominus}$ / kJ mol^{-1}
$As_{(s)}$	+ 302.5
½ $F_{2(g)}$	+ 79.0

a)   Give the definition of standard enthalpy change of atomisation.   (3)

....

....

....

....

b)   Use the equation and the enthalpy change data above to estimate a value
     for the bond energy of the As – F bond.   (3)

E (As – F) = ...kJ mol^{-1}

Total = 6 marks

Question 14

Germanium is an element in Period 4 of the Periodic Table.

a) Write the full electronic structure of germanium. (1)

....

b) Which block of the Periodic Table is germanium found in? .... (1)

Germanium oxide, GeO, is a fairly insoluble white solid.

Enthalpy change	Value / kJ mol^{-1}
$\Delta H_{at}^{\ominus} [Ge_{(s)}]$	+ 376.6
$\Delta H_{at}^{\ominus} [\frac{1}{2} O_{2(g)}]$	+ 124.6
1st ionisation energy of $Ge_{(g)}$, E_{m1}	+ 762
2nd ionisation energy of $Ge_{(g)}$, E_{m2}	+ 1537
$\Delta H_f^{\ominus} [GeO_{(s)}]$	− 212.1
$\Delta H_{aff} [O_{(g)}]$	− 295.4
$\Delta H_{aff} [O^-_{(g)}]$	+ 798

c) Complete the **missing information** in the Born-Haber Cycle and use it to calculate the lattice energy of $GeO_{(s)}$. (9)

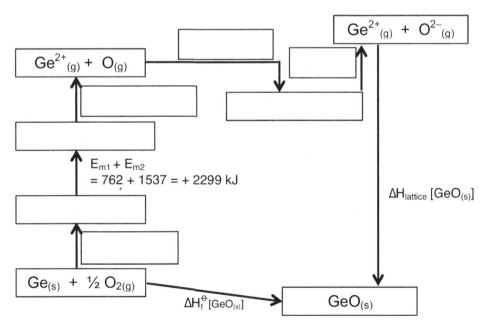

Germanium bromide has the formula $GeBr_4$.

$\Delta H_{at}^{\ominus} [½ Br_{2(l)}] = + 111.9 \text{ kJ mol}^{-1}$

$\Delta H_f^{\ominus} [GeBr_{4(g)}] = - 300.0 \text{ kJ mol}^{-1}$

d)   Use the data above and the $\Delta H_{at}^{\ominus} [Ge_{(s)}]$ used in part c) to calculate a value
     for the bond energy of the Ge – Br bond.   (3)

E (Ge – Br) = ...kJ mol^{-1}

Total = 14 marks

Question 15

Magnesium burns brightly in oxygen with a flame in excess of 2000 °C. This makes direct determination of the enthalpy change of formation for MgO difficult.

The following procedures were carried out to find a value for enthalpy change of the reaction:

$$Mg_{(s)} \quad + \quad \tfrac{1}{2} O_{2(g)} \quad \rightarrow \quad MgO_{(s)}$$

Procedure 1:

1. A strip of magnesium metal was cleaned and the mass measured using a 2 d.p. balance.
2. 50.0 cm^3 of 2.00 mol dm^{-3} HCl$_{(aq)}$ was placed in a polystyrene cup calorimeter and the temperature recorded.
3. The cleaned magnesium metal was cut into small pieces and all of it was added to the HCl$_{(aq)}$.
4. The maximum temperature was recorded.

Procedure 2:

1. 2.00 g of magnesium oxide was collected in a plastic weighing boat.
2. 60.0 cm^3 of 2.00 mol dm^{-3} HCl$_{(aq)}$ was placed in a polystyrene cup calorimeter and the temperature recorded.
3. The magnesium oxide was added to the HCl$_{(aq)}$.
4. The maximum temperature was recorded.

Results

Procedure 1

Mass of Mg$_{(s)}$	= 1.05 g
Initial temperature of the HCl$_{(aq)}$	= 18.5 °C
Maximum temperature of the HCl$_{(aq)}$	= 55.8 °C

Procedure 2

Mass of MgO$_{(s)}$	= 2.05 g
Initial temperature of the HCl$_{(aq)}$	= 20.2 °C
Maximum temperature of the HCl$_{(aq)}$	= 25.0 °C

a) Use the results from the two procedures to calculate the enthalpy change
    for each reaction with $HCl_{(aq)}$ in kJ mol^{-1}.   (8)

Procedure 1	Procedure 2
$\Delta H_{R1} =$	$\Delta H_{R2} =$

b) Add the correct chemical formulae and any balancing numbers to the
    Hess Cycle below to complete the reactions.   (2)

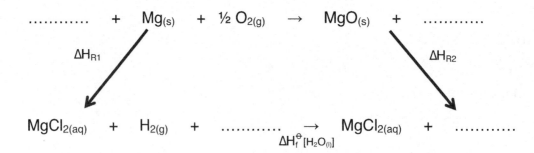

c) Use the Hess Cycle from part b) along with your answers to part a) to calculate a value for $\Delta H_f^\ominus [MgO_{(s)}]$.
Give your answer to a suitable level of accuracy and include a sign. (3)

$\Delta H_f^\ominus [H_2O_{(l)}] = -285.8 \text{ kJ mol}^{-1}$

$\Delta H_f^\ominus [MgO_{(s)}] =$ .... kJ mol^{-1}

The literature value for $\Delta H_f^\ominus [MgO_{(s)}] = -601.7 \text{ kJ mol}^{-1}$.

d) Calculate the percentage difference for your answer to part c) and this literature value. (1)

Percentage difference = ... %

Total = 14 marks

Question 16

Ethanethiol is a chemical that parallels the structure of ethanol but with sulfur replacing the oxygen.

Ethanethiol is a chemical that has a distinctive smell, even at low concentrations in the air and is therefore used to odourise butane and propane fuels.

$\Delta H_f^{\ominus}[CO_{2(g)}] = -393.5$ kJ mol^{-1} $\Delta H_f^{\ominus}[C_2H_5SH_{(l)}] = -73.7$ kJ mol^{-1}

$\Delta H_f^{\ominus}[H_2O_{(l)}] = -285.8$ kJ mol^{-1} $\Delta H_c^{\ominus}[C_2H_5SH_{(l)}] = -2173.2$ kJ mol^{-1}

a)   Add the missing chemical with its balancing number and the missing energy changes to the empty boxes in the Hess Cycle below.   (2)

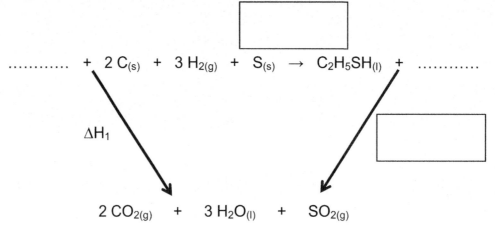

$$\ldots\ldots + \ 2 \ C_{(s)} \ + \ 3 \ H_{2(g)} \ + \ S_{(s)} \ \rightarrow \ C_2H_5SH_{(l)} \ + \ \ldots\ldots$$

ΔH_1

$$2 \ CO_{2(g)} \ + \ 3 \ H_2O_{(l)} \ + \ SO_{2(g)}$$

b)   Give the symbols of the **THREE** enthalpy changes that are added together to make ΔH_1.   (3)

....

c)   Use the Hess Cycle in part a) and the data above to calculate a value for the enthalpy change of formation of sulfur dioxide.

(3)

$\Delta H_f^{\ominus}[SO_{2(g)}] = $ ....kJ mol^{-1}

Total = 8 marks

Question 17

Nitrogen monoxide and nitrogen dioxide are two compounds that exist as free radicals with an unpaired electron on the nitrogen atom.

a)   Draw the dot and cross diagrams for NO and NO_2 molecules.   (4)

NO	NO_2

Nitrogen monoxide will oxidise to form nitrogen dioxide.

b)   Write the balanced equation for the oxidation of nitrogen monoxide.   (1)

....

c)   (i)   Use your dot and cross diagrams and the bond energies below to estimate the enthalpy change for the oxidation of nitrogen monoxide to nitrogen dioxide.   (3)

Bond	Energy / kJ mol^{-1}
N $-$ O	+ 214
N = O	+ 587
N $\equiv$ N	+ 945
O = O	+ 498

ΔH_{R1} = ... kJ mol^{-1}

(ii)   Calculate the enthalpy change for the same reaction using the $\Delta H_f^{\ominus}$ values below.   (1)

Substance	$\Delta H_f^{\ominus}$ / kJ mol^{-1}
$NO_{(g)}$	+ 90.2
$NO_{2(g)}$	+ 33.2

ΔH_{R2} = ... kJ mol^{-1}

(iii)   Comment on the difference between the two values for the oxidation of NO to NO$_2$ referring to the bonding within the molecules. (2)

....

....

....

Nitrogen will react directly with oxygen from the air at the elevated temperatures in an internal combustion engine.

$$N_{2(g)} \quad + \quad O_{2(g)} \quad \rightarrow \quad 2\,NO_{(g)}$$

d)   Calculate a value for the bond energy within nitrogen monoxide using the data above. (3)

$\Delta H_{R3} =$ .... kJ mol^{-1}

e)   Comment on the relative size and signs of the two enthalpy changes (ΔH_{R2} and ΔH_{R3}) and suggest a reason why the direct reaction of nitrogen and oxygen only occurs at elevated temperatures. (2)

....

....

....

....

....

....

....

Total = 16 marks

Question 18

Sodium hydrogen carbonate is the raising agent in baking powder and self-raising flour.

Sodium carbonate can undergo a reaction to become sodium hydrogen carbonate when in contact with carbon dioxide and water.
This limits the shelf life of these products.

$$Na_2CO_{3(s)} + CO_{2(g)} + H_2O_{(l)} \rightarrow 2\,NaHCO_{3(s)} \qquad \Delta H_R = -91.0 \text{ kJ mol}^{-1}$$

a)   Comment on the relative thermal stability of sodium carbonate and sodium hydrogen carbonate. (2)

....

....

....

....

b)   Define the term enthalpy change of formation. (2)

....

....

....

c)   Use the $\Delta H_f^{\ominus}$ data in the table below and the reaction above to calculate a value for the enthalpy change of formation of sodium hydrogen carbonate. Give your answer to an appropriate number of significant figures. (3)

Substance	$\Delta H_f^{\ominus}$ / kJ mol^{-1}
$Na_2CO_{3(s)}$	-1131
$CO_{2(g)}$	-394
$H_2O_{(l)}$	-286

$$\Delta H_f^{\ominus}[NaHCO_{3(s)}] = \text{......................} \text{ kJ mol}^{-1}$$

Total = 7 marks

Question 19

Uranyl nitrate is a compound with the formula $UO_2(NO_3)_2.6H_2O$.

a)   Calculate the percentage by mass of uranium in uranyl nitrate.   (2)

                            Percentage by mass = ...%

Uranyl nitrate undergoes a redox reaction when heated as shown below.

$$2\ UO_2(NO_3)_2.6H_2O_{(s)}\ \rightarrow\ 2\ UO_{3(s)}\ +\ 4\ NO_{2(g)}\ +\ O_{2(g)}\ +\ 6\ H_2O_{(l)}$$

b)   State whether each of the elements below has been oxidised, reduced or
        neither in this decomposition reaction.   (2)

        Uranium ....

        Hydrogen ....

        Oxygen ....

        Nitrogen ....

c)   Use the data below to calculate the enthalpy change for the decomposition
        of uranyl nitrate. Give your answer to 3 significant figures.   (3)

Substance	$\Delta H_f^{\ominus}$ / kJ mol^{-1}
$UO_2(NO_3)_2.6H_2O_{(s)}$	-3198
$UO_{3(s)}$	-1264
$NO_{2(g)}$	$+33.1$
$H_2O_{(l)}$	-285.8

                            ΔH_{dec} = ...kJ mol^{-1}

                                                      Total = 7 marks

Question 20

Phosphorous trichloride can be reacted with chlorine gas to produce phosphorous pentachloride according the reaction below.

$$PCl_{3(l)} + Cl_{2(g)} \rightarrow PCl_{5(s)} \qquad \Delta H_R = \text{exothermic}$$

Data:

$\Delta H_f^{\ominus} [PCl_{3(l)}] = -319.7 \text{ kJ mol}^{-1}$

$\Delta H_f^{\ominus} [Cl_{2(g)}] = 0.0 \text{ kJ mol}^{-1}$

$\Delta H_f^{\ominus} [PCl_{5(s)}] = -443.5 \text{ kJ mol}^{-1}$

$\Delta H_f^{\ominus} [P_{4(s)}] = 0.0 \text{ kJ mol}^{-1}$

a) Why are the $\Delta H_f^{\ominus} [Cl_{2(g)}]$ and $\Delta H_f^{\ominus} [P_{4(s)}]$ values zero? (1)

....

....

....

b) Does the $PCl_{5(s)}$ have more or less energy than the reactants? (1)

....

c) Calculate the value for ΔH_R including a sign and units. (3)

ΔH_R = ... Units: ....

d)   Calculate an alternative value for ΔH_R using the bond energies
       $Cl - Cl = + 243 \text{ kJ mol}^{-1}$ and $P - Cl = + 328 \text{ kJ mol}^{-1}$.   (2)

                              ΔH_R = ... kJ mol^{-1}

e)   Give 2 reasons for the difference between these two values for ΔH_R.   (2)

       Reason 1: ....

       ....

       ....

       ....

       Reason 2: ....

       ....

       ....

       ....

f) Phosphorous trichloride is usually made by reacting white phosphorous with chlorine gas according to the reaction below.

$$P_{4(g)} + 6\ Cl_{2(g)} \rightarrow 4\ PCl_{3(g)} \qquad \Delta H_R = \text{exothermic}$$

Bond Energies:
E (Cl – Cl) = + 243 kJ mol^{-1}

E (P – Cl) = + 328 kJ mol^{-1}

Data:
$\Delta H_f^\ominus$ [PCl$_{3(g)}$] = – 249 kJ mol^{-1}

$\Delta H_f^\ominus$ [P$_{4(g)}$] = + 446 kJ mol^{-1}

(i) Insert the correct numerical values in the enthalpy cycle below. (2)

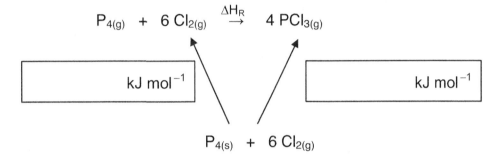

| kJ mol^{-1} | | kJ mol^{-1} |

P$_{4(s)}$ + 6 Cl$_{2(g)}$

(ii) Calculate a value for ΔH_R. (2)

ΔH_R = ... kJ mol^{-1}

(iii) Use the bond energy data and your value for ΔH_R to calculate the bond energy of a P – P bond in the P$_4$ molecule.
Give your answer as a whole number. (3)

(There are 6 P – P bonds in a tetrahedral P$_4$ molecule as shown on the below.)

P$_4$ White Phosophorous

Energy of P – P bond = ... kJ mol^{-1}

Total = 16 marks

Question 21

Propane is used to heat homes and for cooking in rural parts of the country that do not have a direct gas supply.

Propane burns according to the equation below.

$$C_3H_{8(g)} \ + \ 5\,O_{2(g)} \ \rightarrow \ 3\,CO_{2(g)} \ + \ 4\,H_2O_{(l)} \qquad \Delta H_c^\ominus = \text{exothermic}$$

a) State the reason why a combustion reaction MUST be exothermic to be of use in homes. (1)

   ....

   ....

b) Calculate the enthalpy change of combustion using the mean bond energy values listed below. (3)

   Bond Energies:

   $E\ (C-H) \quad = \ +413\ \text{kJ mol}^{-1}$

   $E\ (C-C) \quad = \ +347\ \text{kJ mol}^{-1}$

   $E\ (O=O) \quad = \ +498\ \text{kJ mol}^{-1}$

   $E\ (C=O) \quad = \ +805\ \text{kJ mol}^{-1}$

   $E\ (H-O) \quad = \ +464\ \text{kJ mol}^{-1}$

   $\Delta H_c^\ominus$ = ... kJ mol^{-1}

c) The data book value for $\Delta H_f^\ominus [C_3H_{8(g)}]$ is -2219 kJ mol^{-1}. State the reason for the difference between this value and your calculated answer. (1)

   ....

   ....

d) Calculate the difference as a percentage. (1)

   Percentage difference = ... %

   Total = 6 marks

Question 22

The molecule cyanogen, $(CN)_2$ is described as a pseudo-halogen because in a number of situations it reacts in ways similar to diatomic halogens.

Cyanogen is a colourless gas with the bonding structure shown on the right.

$$N\equiv C-C\equiv N$$

Cyanogen reacts with oxygen in an exothermic reaction.

$$C_2N_{2(g)} + O_{2(g)} \rightarrow 2\,CO_{(g)} + N_{2(g)}$$

a)   Calculate the enthalpy change of combustion using the mean bond energy values listed below.   (3)

Bond Energies:
$E\,(C \equiv N)$ $= +887$ kJ mol^{-1}
$E\,(C - C)$ $= +347$ kJ mol^{-1}
$E\,(O = O)$ $= +498$ kJ mol^{-1}
$E\,(C \equiv O)$ $= +1077$ kJ mol^{-1}
$E\,(N \equiv N)$ $= +945$ kJ mol^{-1}

$\Delta H_c^{\ominus} =$ .... kJ mol^{-1}

The enthalpy change of formation of cyanogen, $\Delta H_f^{\ominus}[(CN)_{2(g)}]$ is $+309.1$ kJ mol^{-1}

b)   Calculate a value for the $\Delta H_f^{\ominus}[(CN)_{2(g)}]$ using the bond energy values.   (3)

$\Delta H_f^{\ominus}[(CN)_{2(g)}] =$ .... kJ mol^{-1}

c) Comment on why the actual value is endothermic rather than the exothermic value you have calculated. (1)

....

....

....

One method to manufacture cyanogen is the dehydration of oxamide in the reaction shown below.

$$H_2N-\overset{O}{\underset{O}{C}}-\overset{O}{C}-NH_2 \longrightarrow (CN)_{2(g)} + 2 H_2O_{(l)}$$

The dehydration of oxamide has an estimated ΔH_R of $+ 116$ kJ mol^{-1}.

Bond Energies:
$E (C \equiv N) = + 887$ kJ mol^{-1}
$E (C - C) = + 347$ kJ mol^{-1}
$E (C - N) = + 286$ kJ mol^{-1}
$E (C = O) = + 805$ kJ mol^{-1}
$E (H - O) = + 464$ kJ mol^{-1}
$E (N - H) = + 391$ kJ mol^{-1}

d) Use the data above to show that the estimated value of ΔH_R for the dehydration of oxamide is $+ 116$ kJ mol^{-1}. (3)

e) State why the published enthalpy change for the reaction will differ from this value. (1)

....

....

....

Total = 11 marks

Question 23

The combustion of ethene in a flow of oxygen gas takes place according to the reaction below.

$$C_2H_{4(g)} + 3 O_{2(g)} \rightarrow 2 CO_{2(g)} + 2 H_2O_{(l)} \qquad \Delta H_R = \text{exothermic}$$

Data:
$\Delta H_f^{\ominus}[C_2H_{4(g)}]$ = + 52.2 kJ mol^{-1} $\Delta H_f^{\ominus}[CO_{2(g)}]$ = − 393.5 kJ mol^{-1}

$\Delta H_f^{\ominus}[O_{2(g)}]$ = 0.0 kJ mol^{-1} $\Delta H_f^{\ominus}[H_2O_{(l)}]$ = − 285.8 kJ mol^{-1}

a)   State why the $\Delta H_f^{\ominus}[O_{2(g)}]$ has a value of zero? (1)

....

....

....

b)   Will the products have more or less energy than the reactants? (1)

....

c)   Complete the enthalpy cycle with the missing substances with state symbols and labels (no numerical enthalpy values are required). (2)

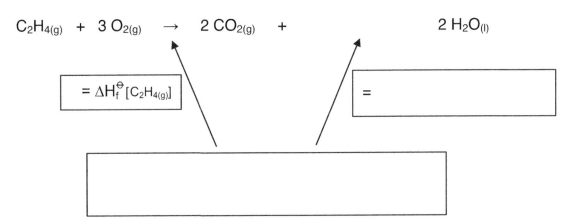

$$C_2H_{4(g)} + 3 O_{2(g)} \rightarrow 2 CO_{2(g)} + \qquad\qquad 2 H_2O_{(l)}$$

= $\Delta H_f^{\ominus}[C_2H_{4(g)}]$

=

d)   Calculate the value for ΔH_R including a sign and units. (2)

ΔH_R = ... Units: ....

Total = 6 marks

Question 24

It is often difficult to carry out the reaction to determine the enthalpy change of formation of a substance directly. The formation of methane is an example.

a)   Complete the equation, including state symbols, that represents the enthalpy change of formation of methane.   (2)

.... $\rightarrow$ $CH_{4(g)}$

Data:

$\Delta H_c^\ominus [CH_{4(g)}]$ = -890.3 kJ mol^{-1}

$\Delta H_c^\ominus [H_{2(g)}]$ = -285.8 kJ mol^{-1}

$\Delta H_c^\ominus [C_{(s, graphite)}]$ = -393.5 kJ mol^{-1}

b)   Construct an enthalpy cycle using the $\Delta H_c^\ominus$ values by including $O_{2(g)}$ to confirm that the $\Delta H_f^\ominus [CH_{4(g)}]$ has a value of -74.8 kJ mol^{-1}.   (3)

The unlikely reaction shown below converts methane into ethane.

$$2\ CH_{4(g)} \quad \rightarrow \quad C_2H_{6(g)} \quad + \quad H_{2(g)}$$

c)   Use the enthalpy changes of formation of methane and ethane to calculate a value for the enthalpy change of this conversion.   (2)

$\Delta H_f^\ominus [C_2H_{6(g)}] = -84.7$ kJ mol^{-1}

ΔH_R = ...kJ mol^{-1}

Total = 7 marks

Question 25

Anhydrous aluminium chloride will absorb water and become hydrated aluminium chloride according to the equation below.

$$AlCl_{3(s)} \quad + \quad 6\,H_2O_{(l)} \quad \rightarrow \quad AlCl_3.6H_2O_{(s)}$$

Data:

$\Delta H_f^{\ominus}[AlCl_{3(s)}] \quad = \quad -704.2 \text{ kJ mol}^{-1}$

$\Delta H_f^{\ominus}[AlCl_3.6H_2O_{(s)}] \quad = \quad -2691.6 \text{ kJ mol}^{-1}$

$\Delta H_f^{\ominus}[H_2O_{(l)}] \quad = \quad -285.8 \text{ kJ mol}^{-1}$

$\Delta H_f^{\ominus}[Al(OH)_{3(s)}] \quad = \quad -1287.4 \text{ kJ mol}^{-1}$

$\Delta H_f^{\ominus}[HCl_{(g)}] \quad = \quad -92.3 \text{ kJ mol}^{-1}$

a) Calculate a value for the enthalpy change when anhydrous aluminium chloride reacts with water.
Give you answer to an appropriate number of significant figures. (3)

$$\Delta H_R = \text{.......................................} \text{ kJ mol}^{-1}$$

b) Would you expect the solid aluminium chloride to rise or fall in temperature as this reaction takes place? (1)

....

Heating hydrated aluminium chloride, $AlCl_3.6H_2O_{(s)}$, results in the thermal decomposition shown below taking place.

$$AlCl_3.6H_2O_{(s)} \rightarrow Al(OH)_{3(s)} + 3 H_2O_{(l)} + 3 HCl_{(g)}$$

c) Why would it be difficult to determine a value for the enthalpy change for this reaction by experiment? (1)

....

....

....

d) (i) Given that you have to heat the $AlCl_3.6H_2O_{(s)}$ to cause the decomposition, would you expect the reaction to be exothermic or endothermic? (1)

....

(ii) Selecting from the data above, calculate a value for the enthalpy change for the decomposition of $AlCl_3.6H_2O_{(s)}$ as shown in the reaction above. Give your answer to an appropriate number of significant figures. (3)

$\Delta H_R =$ ....kJ mol^{-1}

Total = 9 marks

Question 26

There are a wide variety of potential biofuels.

One candidate is ethyl valerate (ethyl pentanoate), an ester that has an apple-like odour that is derived from the processing of plant materials.

Ethyl pentanoate has the formula $C_7H_{14}O_2$.

a) Confirm that the analysis below matches the formula of
    ethyl pentanoate.   (3)

   A 2.050 g sample of ethyl pentanoate was combusted in pure oxygen.

   Mass of CO_2 formed = 4.857 g

   Mass of H_2O formed = 1.987 g

Ethyl pentanoate can be formed from reacting pentanoic acid with ethanol according to the reaction below.

$$C_5H_9O_2H_{(l)} \quad + \quad C_2H_5OH_{(l)} \quad \rightarrow \quad C_7H_{14}O_{2(l)} \quad + \quad H_2O_{(l)}$$

Data:

$\Delta H_R \qquad = \quad -4.6 \text{ kJ mol}^{-1}$ $\qquad\qquad \Delta H_f^{\ominus}[H_2O_{(l)}] \quad = \quad -285.8 \text{ kJ mol}^{-1}$

$\Delta H_f^{\ominus}[C_5H_9O_2H_{(l)}] = \quad -557.8 \text{ kJ mol}^{-1}$ $\qquad \Delta H_f^{\ominus}[CO_{2(l)}] \quad = \quad -393.5 \text{ kJ mol}^{-1}$

$\Delta H_f^{\ominus}[C_2H_5OH_{(g)}] = \quad -277.1 \text{ kJ mol}^{-1}$

b) Use the data above to calculate a value for the $\Delta H_f^{\ominus}[C_7H_{14}O_{2(s)}]$.   (3)

$$\Delta H_f^{\ominus}[C_7H_{14}O_{2(s)}] = \quad \text{......................} \quad \text{kJ mol}^{-1}$$

c) Complete the equation for the combustion of ethyl pentanoate. (2)

$$C_7H_{14}O_{2(l)} \quad + \quad \text{......} \; O_{2(g)} \quad \rightarrow \quad \text{......} \; CO_{2(g)} \quad + \quad \text{......} \; H_2O_{(l)}$$

d) Use your answer to part c) along with data selected from above to calculate a value for the enthalpy change of combustion of ethyl pentanoate, $\Delta H_c^{\ominus}[C_7H_{14}O_{2(s)}]$.
Give your answer to 4 significant figures. (3)

e) Explain the following terms.

Biofuel (1)

....

....

....

Drop-in biofuel (1)

....

....

....

Explain why biofuels are **not** the answer to the problems of fossil fuels. (2)

....

....

....

....

....

Total = 15 marks

Question 27

An experiment to determine the enthalpy change of combustion of cyclohexane was carried out using the equipment shown on the right.

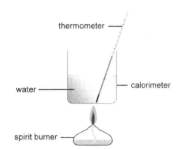

The results obtained are listed below.

Mass of burner before combustion.................................... 42.56 g

Mass of burner after combustion.................................... 40.76 g

Mass of cyclohexane burned .... **g**

Mass of water in the beaker .... 402 g

Temperature at the water at the start............................ 15.2 °C

Temperature of water after the combustion .... 52.2 °C

Temperature change... **°C**

a) Calculate the missing values for mass change and temperature change, giving your answers to an appropriate number of significant figures. (1)

b) Calculate the energy released (Q) from burning the cyclohexane. (1)

Q = ...J

c) Calculate the number of moles of cyclohexane burned.
(M_r(cyclohexane) = 84.0) (1)

Moles of cyclohexane = ... moles

d) Combine your answers to parts b) and c) to find the $\Delta H_c^{\ominus}$ of cyclohexane in kJ mol^{-1}.
Give your answer to an appropriate number of significant figures. (2)

$\Delta H_c^{\ominus}$ = ... kJ mol^{-1}

e) The expected value for the $\Delta H_c^\ominus$ of cyclohexane is -3920 kJ mol^{-1}.
Calculate the percentage difference for your answer to part d). (1)

Percentage difference = ...%

The uncertainty of the various pieces of equipment is shown in the table below.

Equipment	Uncertainty	Times used	Value measured	Percentage uncertainty
Thermometer	± 0.05 °C			%
500 cm^3 measuring cylinder	± 5 cm^3	1	400 cm^3	%
Balance	± 0.005 g	2		%
Total Percentage Uncertainty =				%

f) Insert or calculate the missing values in the table. (4)

g) Using your **total percentage uncertainty** from part f), calculate the range that your value from part d) could have. (2)

Range of Enthalpy Change:

(More negative) Minimum value for $\Delta H_c^\ominus$ = ... kJ mol^{-1}

(More positive) Maximum value for $\Delta H_c^\ominus$ = ... kJ mol^{-1}

The value obtained in part d) lies outside the range calculated in part g).

h) State **three** significant errors in the method of combustion used. (3)

Error 1: ....

Error 2: ....

Error 3: ....

Total = 15 marks

Question 28

An experiment was carried out to find the enthalpy change of combustion for ethylamine.

A jet of ethylamine was burned underneath an aluminium can containing 350 g of water.

The volume of ethylamine gas was used to find the number of moles burned under the can.

The results are shown below.

Volume of ethylamine burned (at RTP) ....387 cm^3

Mass of water in the beaker ....350 g

Temperature of the water at the start........................17.5 °C

Temperature of the water after the combustion.........33.7 °C

a)   Show by calculation that the experimental value for the enthalpy change of combustion, $\Delta H_c^\ominus$ of ethylamine was −1470 kJ mol^{-1}.   (4)

   1 mole of gas occupies 24.0 dm^3 at 298K and 100kPa.

A similar experiment was performed using both hex-1-ene and cyclohexane in spirit burners. Both of these compounds have the same molecular formula, C_6H_{12}.

The values obtained for $\Delta H_c^\ominus$ were -3620 kJ mol^{-1} and -3520 kJ mol^{-1} respectively.

b)   Suggest a reason related to the structure of the substances why the values for $\Delta H_c^\ominus$ were not the same. (1)

....

....

....

c)   Give **a major reason** why the actual data source values for $\Delta H_c^\ominus$ for both compounds are notably more exothermic than these values. (1)

....

....

Total = 6 marks

Question 29

Manganese is an important metal that is used in a range of hard steels.

Manganese occurs in a range of oxides, two of which are manganese(II) oxide (MnO) and manganese(IV) oxide (MnO_2).

$$2\ MnO_{(s)}\ +\ O_{2(g)}\ \xrightarrow{\Delta H_R}\ 2\ MnO_{2(s)}\qquad \Delta H_R = \text{exothermic}$$

Data:

$\Delta H_f^{\ominus} [MnO_{(s)}]\quad = \quad -385.2\ kJ\ mol^{-1}$

$\Delta H_f^{\ominus} [O_{2(g)}]\quad = \qquad 0.0\ kJ\ mol^{-1}$

$\Delta H_f^{\ominus} [MnO_{2(s)}]\quad = \quad -520.0\ kJ\ mol^{-1}$

a)   State the definition of the term "*enthalpy change of formation*".   (2)

....

....

....

....

b)   Explain why the value in the data for oxygen is zero.   (1)

....

....

c)   Complete the energy cycle with the correct substances.
Use this cycle to calculate a value for ΔH_R, the enthalpy change for the reaction.
Give your answer to an appropriate number of significant figures.   (4)

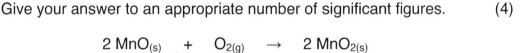

$$2\ MnO_{(s)}\quad +\quad O_{2(g)}\quad \longrightarrow\quad 2\ MnO_{2(s)}$$

_____

Elements

Value for ΔH_R = ... kJ mol^{-1}

Total = 7 marks

Question 30

Pentan-1-ol is a flammable liquid alcohol with the formula $CH_3CH_2CH_2CH_2CH_2OH$

a)   Complete the balanced equation for the complete combustion of 1 mole of
      pentan-1-ol.   (1)

$$C_5H_{11}OH_{(l)} \quad + \quad \ldots\ldots O_{2(g)} \quad \rightarrow \quad \ldots\ldots CO_{2(g)} \quad + \quad \ldots\ldots H_2O_{(l)}$$

A sample of pentan-1-ol was burned in a can calorimeter as shown on the right.

Mass of water used	400.00 g
Temperature rise	24.5 °C
Mass of spirit burner with pentan-1-ol before burning / g	128.44
Mass of spirit burner with pentan-1-ol after burning / g	127.04
Mass of $C_5H_4O_2$ burned / g	
M_r [$C_5H_{11}OH_{(l)}$]	88.0

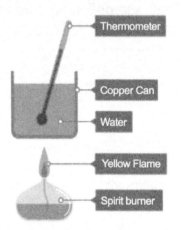

b)   Complete the missing data in the table above, giving the value to an
      appropriate number of significant figures.   (1)

c)   Calculate the experimental value for $\Delta H_c^\ominus$ [$C_5H_{11}OH_{(l)}$] from the data above.
      Give your answer to an appropriate number of significant figures and
      include a sign with your answer.   (4)

      Specific heat capacity of water = 4.18 J K^{-1} g^{-1}

$\Delta H_c^\ominus$ [$C_5H_{11}OH_{(l)}$] = ... kJ mol^{-1}

d) The accepted value for $\Delta H_c^{\ominus}[C_5H_{11}OH_{(l)}] = -3329.0$ kJ mol^{-1}. Calculate the percentage difference from the experimental value.
Give your answer to 3 significant figures. (1)

Percentage error = ... %

The pieces of equipment used in the experiment have the following uncertainties.

Equipment	Uncertainty	Percentage uncertainty
Thermometer to measure the temperature rise	± 0.05 °C	
Mass change of burner	± 0.005 g	
Balance to measure water mass	± 0.005 g	± 0.0025 %

e) Calculate the missing data in the table above remembering to incorporate the number of times the equipment is used to generate the reading. (2)

f) Calculate the total percentage uncertainty for the experimental procedure. (1)

Total percentage uncertainty = ... %

g) Calculate the uncertainty in kJ mol^{-1} and state the experimental value of $\Delta H_c^{\ominus}$ including this uncertainty. (1)

Experimental value for $\Delta H_c^{\ominus}[C_5H_{11}OH_{(l)}]$ = ... ± .... kJ mol^{-1}

h) State a change to the procedure that would reduce the **TWO** most significant uncertainties. Explain your answer. (3)

Change: ....

Explanation: ....

....

....

....

Total = 14 marks

Question 31

Propene cannot be formed directly from carbon and hydrogen in a reaction. However, a value for $\Delta H_f^{\ominus}$ can be calculated using an enthalpy cycle.

Substance	$\Delta H_c^{\ominus}$ / kJ mol^{-1}
$C_{(s, \text{ graphite})}$	-393.5
$H_{2(g)}$	-285.8
$C_3H_{6(g)}$	-2058

a) Complete **ALL** of the details and labelling of a suitable enthalpy cycle to calculate a value for $\Delta H_f^{\ominus}[C_3H_{6(g)}]$ starting with the equation shown below.

(4)

Enthalpy Cycle:

$$3\ C_{(s, \text{ graphite})} \quad + \quad 3\ H_{2(g)} \quad \rightarrow \quad C_3H_{6(g)}$$

Calculation of enthalpy change of formation of propene:

$$\Delta H_f^{\ominus}[C_3H_{6(g)}] = \text{.............................} \text{ kJ mol}^{-1}$$

Propene will react with HBr to form 1-bromopropane and 2-bromopropane, which both have the same molecular formula.

$$C_3H_{6(g)} \quad + \quad Br_{2(l)} \quad \rightarrow \quad C_3H_5Br_{(l)}$$

Substance	Boiling point / K	$\Delta H_f^{\ominus}$ / kJ mol^{-1}
$CH_3CH_2CH_2Br_{(l)}$	344	-116.4
$CH_3CHBrCH_{3(l)}$	333	-128.5
$HBr_{(g)}$	206	-36.4

b)   Explain why the boiling points of 1-bromopropane and 2-bromopropane
      are not the same?   (2)

      ....

      ....

      ....

      ....

c)   Use your value for $\Delta H_f^\ominus [C_3H_{6(g)}]$ from part a) and the $\Delta H_f^\ominus$ data on the
      previous page to calculate the enthalpy change for the reaction to form
      1-bromopropane and 2-bromopropane separately.
      Give your answers to 1 decimal place.   (4)

1-bromopropane	2-bromopropane
$C_3H_{6(g)} + HBr_{(g)} \rightarrow CH_3CH_2CH_2Br_{(l)}$	$C_3H_{6(g)} + HBr_{(g)} \rightarrow CH_3CHBrCH_{3(l)}$
$\Delta H_R =$ .... kJ mol^{-1}	$\Delta H_R =$ .... kJ mol^{-1}

d) (i) State why the ΔH_R values for the two isomeric products are similar. (1)

....

....

....

....

....

(ii) State why the ΔH_R for the two isomeric products is **not** identical. (1)

....

....

....

....

....

....

Total = 12 marks

Question 32

Bond energies can be used to give an estimate of the enthalpy change for a reaction.

Solid glucose will burn in a supply of oxygen to form carbon dioxide and water.

$$+ \quad 6\,O_{2(g)} \quad \rightarrow \quad 6\,CO_{2(g)} \quad + \quad 6\,H_2O_{(l)}$$

Bond Energy Data:

$E\,(C-H) \quad = \quad +413 \text{ kJ mol}^{-1}$

$E\,(C-C) \quad = \quad +347 \text{ kJ mol}^{-1}$

$E\,(C-O) \quad = \quad +358 \text{ kJ mol}^{-1}$

$E\,(O=O) \quad = \quad +498 \text{ kJ mol}^{-1}$

$E\,(C=O) \quad = \quad +805 \text{ kJ mol}^{-1}$

$E\,(O-H) \quad = \quad +464 \text{ kJ mol}^{-1}$

a) Calculate an estimated value for the $\Delta H_c^{\ominus}[C_6H_{12}O_{6(s)}]$ in kJ mol^{-1}. (5)

Break: (Glucose has 24 bonds in its structure)	Make:

$$\Delta H_c^{\ominus}[C_6H_{12}O_{6(s)}] = \ \text{........................} \ \text{kJ mol}^{-1}$$

b) Give **TWO** reasons why this estimated value is not identical to the
published value for the combustion of glucose of $-2802.5 \text{ kJ mol}^{-1}$.   (2)

Reason 1:..

....

Reason 2: ....

....

Total = 7 marks

Question 33

Bond energies, $E(X - Z)$ are defined as the enthalpy change for breaking 1 mole of a bond into separate atoms in the gaseous state.

The enthalpy change of formation for a compound is defined as the enthalpy change for forming 1 mole of a compound under standard conditions from its constituent elements in their standard states.

Bond Energy Data:

$E (C - H)$ $= + 435$ kJ mol^{-1}

$E (C - Br)$ $= + 285$ kJ mol^{-1}

$E (C \equiv N)$ $= + 887$ kJ mol^{-1}

$E (C - C)$ $= + 347$ kJ mol^{-1}

a)   Use the bond energy data above to estimate the bond energy of the $H - Br$ bond by using the reaction shown below.   (4)

$$CH_3Br_{(g)} + HCN_{(g)} \rightarrow CH_3CN_{(g)} + HBr_{(g)} \qquad \Delta H_R = - 10 \text{ kJ mol}^{-1}$$

$E(H - Br) = $ .... kJ mol^{-1}

1,2-dichloroethane undergoes thermal cracking to form chloroethene in the reaction below.

$$CH_2ClCH_2Cl_{(g)} \rightarrow CH_2 = CHCl_{(g)} + HCl_{(g)} \qquad \Delta H_R = -285 \text{ kJ mol}^{-1}$$

b) Use the bond energy data listed below to estimate a value for the enthalpy change of formation of chloroethene, $\Delta H_f^\ominus [CH_2 = CHCl_{(g)}]$. (4)

Data:

E (H − H)	= + 436 kJ mol^{-1}	E (C − H)	= + 413 kJ mol^{-1}
E (Cl − Cl)	= + 243 kJ mol^{-1}	E (C − Cl)	= + 346 kJ mol^{-1}
E (C − C)	= + 347 kJ mol^{-1}		
E (C = C)	= + 612 kJ mol^{-1}	$\Delta H_{at}^\ominus [C_{(s,\ graphite)}]$	= + 716.7 kJ mol^{-1}

$\Delta H_f^\ominus [CH_2 = CHCl_{(g)}] = $ .... kJ mol^{-1}

Total = 8 marks

Question 34

When acids react with alkalis there is an exothermic enthalpy change.

One factor in the magnitude of this energy change is the strength of the acid.

In this question, you should give each numerical answer to an approriate number of significant figures.

Neutralisation 1:

When 75.0 cm^3 of 0.800 mol dm^{-3} $H_2SO_{4(aq)}$ is neutralised by 240.0 cm^3 of 0.500 mol dm^{-3} $NaOH_{(aq)}$ the mixture rises in temperature by 5.2 °C.

a)   Write the full balanced equation for this neutralisation.   (2)

....

b)   Show that neither chemical is in excess.   (2)

c)   Use your answers to parts a) and b) to calculate $\Delta H^{\ominus}_{neut}$ for **Neutralisation 1** per mole of sulfuric acid.   (2)

$$\Delta H^{\ominus}_{neut} = \text{.................................... kJ mol}^{-1}$$

Neutralisation 2:

When $HCl_{(aq)}$ is neutralised by $NaOH_{(aq)}$ the $\Delta H^{\ominus}_{neut} = -57.9$ kJ mol^{-1}.

d) Estimate the recorded temperature rise when 25.0 cm^3 of 0.500 mol dm^{-3} $HCl_{(aq)}$ is neutralised by 25.0 cm^3 of 0.500 mol dm^{-3} $NaOH_{(aq)}$. (3)

Estimated temperature rise = ... °C

Neutralisation 3:

e) Explain why when ethanoic acid is used instead of sulfuric or hydrochloric acid, the value of $\Delta H^{\ominus}_{neut}$ is less exothermic (smaller in magnitude). (3)

....

....

....

....

....

....

....

....

Total = 12 marks

Question 35

The conversion of rubidium hydrogen carbonate into rubidium carbonate is impossible to achieve.

$$2\ RbHCO_{3(s)} \quad \rightarrow \quad Rb_2CO_{3(s)} \quad + \quad CO_{2(g)} \quad + \quad H_2O_{(l)}$$

To determine a value for the enthalpy change of this reaction, two experiments were carried out.

Procedure 1:
A 4.62 g sample of $Rb_2CO_{3(s)}$ was added to 100.0 cm^3 of 0.5 mol dm^{-3} HCl (an excess).
The temperature of the solution rose by 2.2 °C.

Procedure 2:
A 4.40 g sample of $RbHCO_{3(s)}$ was added to 100.0 cm3 of 0.5 mol dm–3 (an excess).
The temperature of the solution fell by 2.3 °C.

a) Calculate the enthalpy change for the conversion of $RbHCO_{3(s)}$ into $Rb_2CO_{3(s)}$ in the reaction above.
    Give your answer to an appropriate number of significant figures and include a sign with your calculated value. (8)

b) Given your answer to part a), comment on the relative thermal stability of $RbHCO_3$ and Rb_2CO_3 and what would happen to either over a long period of time. (2)

....

....

....

Total = 10 marks

Question 36

A common Hess Cycle links enthalpy changes for solution, lattice energy and the hydration of ions

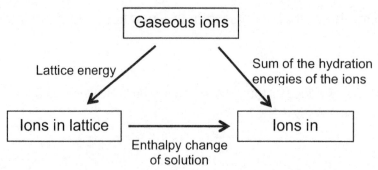

a) Use the data to calculate the enthalpy change of solution for sodium bromide._ (2)

Substance	$\Delta H_{Hydration}$ / kJ mol^{-1}	$\Delta H_{Lattice}$ / kJ mol^{-1}
NaBr	n/a	-742
Na$^{+}_{(g)}$	-405	n/a
Br$^{-}_{(g)}$	-348	n/a

$\Delta H^{\ominus}_{solution}$ = ...kJ mol^{-1}

b) Given your answer to part a), calculate the expected temperature change when dissolving 14.7 g of NaBr in 250 g of water. (3)

Specific heat capacity of water = 4.18 J K^{-1} g^{-1}

Temperature change = ... °C

Total = 5 marks

Question 37

Substance M is soluble in water. It has the formula MF_2.

Dissolving 0.0550 moles of **substance M** in 255.0 g of water causes the temperature of the water to fall by 0.86 °C.

a) Calculate the $\Delta H^{\ominus}_{solution}$ of **substance M**.
    Give your answer to an appropriate number of significant figures.   (3)

    Specific heat capacity of water = 4.18 J K^{-1} g^{-1}

$$\Delta H^{\ominus}_{solution} = \text{.................................. kJ mol}^{-1}$$

b) Complete the Hess Cycle below by filling in the missing information and chemical species.   (2)

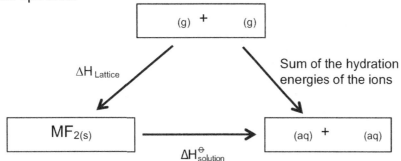

Substance	$\Delta H_{Hydration}$ / kJ mol^{-1}	$\Delta H_{Lattice}$ / kJ mol^{-1}
$MF_{2(s)}$		− 1755
$F^{-}_{(g)}$	− 524	

c) Use your answer to part a) and the data above to calculate the hydration energy of the ion of the **metal M**. Give your answer to an appropriate number of significant figures.   (3)

$$\Delta H^{\ominus}_{hydration} = \text{........................... kJ mol}^{-1}$$

Total = 8 marks

Question 38

Strontium iodide has the formula SrI_2.

a) Use the data below to calculate a value for the lattice energy of SrI_2 using a Hess Cycle. (3)

Substance	$\Delta H_{Hydration}$ / kJ mol^{-1}	$\Delta H_{Solution}$ / kJ mol^{-1}
$SrI_{2(s)}$	n/a	-70.0
$I^-_{(g)}$	-295	n/a
$Sr^{2+}_{(g)}$	-1443	n/a

$\Delta H^{\ominus}_{Lattice}[SrI_2] =$ .... kJ mol^{-1}

b) Use the value of $\Delta H_{solution}$ for strontium iodide to calculate the expected change in temperature if 4.3 g of SrI_2 was dissolved in 250 cm^3 of water. State whether it is a rise or fall in temperature. (4)

[Specific heat capacity of $H_2O_{(l)} = 4.18$ J g^{-1} K^{-1}]

Temperature change = ... °C

Total = 7 marks

Answers

Do not round answers during calculations, write down your on-going answers with too many significant figures. Only round your final answer to the correct number of significant figures as explained below.

In working out answers it is worth remembering the following M_r values.

$H_2O = 18.0$	$O_3 = 48.0$	$SO_4 = 96.1$ $(32.1 + 4\times16)$
$OH = 17.0$	$O_4 = 64.0$	$CO_3 = 60.0$ $(12 + 3\times16)$
$CO_2 = 44.0$	$Cl_2 = 71.0$	$NO_3 = 62.0$ $(14 + 3\times16)$

In all answers, the number of significant figures is determined by the least accurate piece of data within the question. This may be the A_r value from a periodic table.

250 is 2 s.f.   250.0 is 4 s.f.   0.00250 is 3 s.f.   0.000025 is 2 s.f.

Questions To Test Your Knowledge – Part 1

Question 1		Equation: $ZnCl_{2(aq)} + Mg_{(s)} \rightarrow MgCl_{2(aq)} + Zn_{(s)}$
		Moles of $ZnCl_2$ = 0.5 x 40 / 1000 = 0.0200 mol
		Moles of Mg = 0.405 / 24.3 = 0.016667 mol
		Limiting reagent is Mg
		Q = 40.0 x 4.18 x 1.6 = 267.52 J
		ΔH_R = 267.52 / 0.016667 = 16051 J $= -$ **16 kJ mol^{-1} to 2 s.f.** (Temperature is 2 s.f.)
Question 2	a)	Moles of HCl = 0.250 x 50 / 1000 = 0.0125
		Moles of $NaHCO_3$ = 5.00 / (23 + 1 + 60) = 0.0595 mol
		Fewer moles of HCl (in a 1:1 reaction) so this is limiting reagent
	b)	ΔH_R = 100.0 x 4.18 x 4.5 / 0.0125 = 150,480 $= +$ **150 kJ mol^{-1} to 2 s.f.**
Question 3	a)	Moles of HNO_3 = 0.250 x 50.0 / 1000 = 0.0125
		Moles of K_2CO_3 = 0.400 x 50.0 / 1000 = 0.0200 mol
		Equation: $K_2CO_{3(aq)} + 2\ HNO_{3(aq)} \rightarrow 2\ KNO_{3(aq)} + CO_{2(g)} + H_2O_{(l)}$
		0.0125 moles of HNO_3 needs 0.00625 moles of K_2CO_3 so nitric acid is limiting reagent
	b)	ΔH_R = (50.0+50.0) x 4.18 x 8.4 / 0.0125 = 280,890 $= -$ **280 kJ mol^{-1} to 2 s.f.**
Question 4	a)	Reaction is 1:1
		Moles of both NaOH and HCl = 0.250 x 50.0 / 1000 = 0.0125 mol
		ΔH_R = (50.0+50.0) x 4.18 x 1.7 / 0.0125 = 56,848 $= -$ **57 kJ mol^{-1} to 2 s.f.**
Question 5	a)	480 cm^3 of ethene = 480 / 24000 = 0.0200 moles
		ΔH = 400.0 x 4.18 x 10.6 / 0.0200 = 886,160 J mol^{-1} $= -$ **886 kJ mol^{-1}**
	b)	Incomplete combustion **AND** heat not captured by the water
	c)	Percentage difference = 100 x (1411 − 886) / 1411 = **37.2 %**

Question 6	a)	Moles of propanone = 1.160 / 58 = 0.0200 mol ΔH = 445 x 4.18 x 13.3 / 0.0200 = 1,236,967 J mol^{-1} ΔH = **– 1240 kJ mol^{-1} to 3 s.f.**
	b)	Percentage difference = 100 x (1816.5 – 1240) / 1816.5 = **31.7 %**
Question 7	a)	Moles of octan-1-ol = 0.650 / 130 = 0.00500 mol 5293.6 x 1000 = 400.0 x 4.18 x ΔT / 0.00500 ΔT = 5293.6 x 1000 x 0.00500 / (400 x 4.18) = **15.8 °C rise**
	b)	Incomplete combustion **AND** heat not captured by the water

Questions To Test Your Knowledge – Part 2

Question 8		ΔH_R = + 74.8 + 241.8 + – 110.5 = **+ 206.6 kJ mol^{-1}**
Question 9		ΔH_R = 2 x + 2154.8 + 2 x – 592.0 + 4 x + 33.2 + 8 x –241.8 ΔH_R = 4309.6 – 1184 + 132.8 – 1934.4 = **+ 1324.0 kJ mol^{-1}**
Question 10		ΔH_R = + 566.9 + 3 x 285.8 + – 1675.7 + 3 x + 29.7 ΔH_R = + 566.9 + 857.4 – 1675.7 + 89.1 = **– 162.3 kJ mol^{-1}**
Question 11		ΔH_R = – $\Delta H_f^{\ominus}$[CS$_2$] + $\Delta H_f^{\ominus}$[CO$_2$] + 2 $\Delta H_f^{\ominus}$[SO$_2$] $\Delta H_f^{\ominus}$[CS$_2$] = $\Delta H_f^{\ominus}$[CO$_2$] + 2 $\Delta H_f^{\ominus}$[SO$_2$] – ΔH_R = – 393.5 + 2 x – 296.8 – – 1076.8 $\Delta H_f^{\ominus}$[CS$_2$] = **+ 89.7 kJ mol^{-1}**
Question 12		ΔH_R = – 2 $\Delta H_f^{\ominus}$[TlOH] – $\Delta H_f^{\ominus}$[CO$_2$] + $\Delta H_f^{\ominus}$[Tl$_2$CO$_3$] + $\Delta H_f^{\ominus}$[H$_2$O] $\Delta H_f^{\ominus}$[Tl$_2$CO$_3$] = ΔH_R + 2 $\Delta H_f^{\ominus}$[TlOH] + $\Delta H_f^{\ominus}$[CO$_2$] – $\Delta H_f^{\ominus}$[H$_2$O] $\Delta H_f^{\ominus}$[Tl$_2$CO$_3$] = – 488.1 + 2 x – 104.2 + – 393.5 + 285.8 = **– 804.2 kJ mol^{-1}**

Question 13		*Long method:* Break: 6(C − H) + 1(C − C) + 1(C = C) + 1(Cl − Cl) = 6x413 + 347 + 612 + 243 = + 3680 kJ mol^{-1} Make: 6(C − H) + 2(C − C) + 2(C − Cl) = 6x413 + 2x347 + 2x346 = − 3864 kJ mol^{-1} Overall: ΔH = + 3680 − 3864 = **− 184 kJ mol^{-1}** *Short method:* Break: 1(C = C) + 1(Cl − Cl) = 612 + 243 = + 855 kJ mol^{-1} Make: 1(C − C) + 2(C − Cl) = 347 + 2x346 = −1039 kJ mol^{-1} Overall: ΔH = + 855 − 1039 = **− 184 kJ mol^{-1}**
Question 14	a)	*Long method:* Break: 2(C = O) + 2(C − O) + 1(C − C) + 2(O − H) + ½(O = O) = 2x805 + 2x358 + 347 + 2x464 + ½x498 = + 3850 kJ mol^{-1} Make: 4(C = O) + 2(H − O) = 4x805 + 2x464 = − 4148 kJ mol^{-1} Overall = +3850 − 4148 = **− 298 kJ mol^{-1}** *Short method:* Break: 2(C − O) + 1(C − C) + ½(O = O) = 2 x 358 + 347 + ½x498 = + 1312 kJ mol^{-1} Make: 2(C = O) = 2x805 = − 1610 kJ mol^{-1} Overall = +1312 − 1610 = **− 298 kJ mol^{-1}**
	b)	Bond energies are mean values and vary between actual compounds for the same bond. Bond energies are for the gaseous state but ethanedioic acid is a solid and water a liquid in the equation.

Question 15	a)	$\Delta H_R = +\ 774.9 + 2\times 241.8 - 296.8 - 4\times 271.1$ $= -\ \textbf{122.7 kJ mol}^{-1}$
	b)	Break: $4(S - F) + 4(O - H)$ $= 4E + 4\times 464 = 4E + 1856\ \text{kJ mol}^{-1}$ Make: $2(S = O) + 4(H - F)$ $= 2\times 523 + 4\times 568 = -\ 3318\ \text{kJ mol}^{-1}$ Overall: $4E + 1856 - 3318 = -122.7\ \text{kJ mol}^{-1}$ $4E = -\ 122.7 - 1856 + 3318 = +\ 1339.3\ \text{kJ mol}^{-1}$ $E(S - F) = +\ 334.825 = +\ \textbf{335 kJ mol}^{-1}$
Question 16		Adding 4 O_2 to the enthalpy cycle for the combustion of C_3H_6O $\Delta H_f^{\ominus}[C_3H_6O_{(l)}]$ $3\ C_{(s)} + 3\ H_{2(g)} + 4\tfrac{1}{2}\ O_{2(g)} \rightarrow C_3H_6O_{(l)} + 4\ O_{2(g)}$ $3\times\Delta H_c^{\ominus}[C_{(s,\ graphite)}]$ $+\ 3\times\Delta H_c^{\ominus}[H_{2(g)}]$ $\Delta H_c^{\ominus}[C_3H_6O_{(l)}]$ $3\ CO_{2(g)} + 3\ H_2O_{(l)}$ $\Delta H_c^{\ominus}[C_3H_6O_{(l)}] = -\ \Delta H_f^{\ominus}[C_3H_6O_{(l)}] + 3\ \Delta H_c^{\ominus}[C_{(s,\ graphite)}] + 3\ \Delta H_c^{\ominus}[H_{2(g)}]$ $\Delta H_c^{\ominus}[C_3H_6O_{(l)}] = +\ 248.0 + 3\ \times -\ 393.5 + 3\ \times -\ 285.8 = 248.0 - 1180.5 - 857.4$ $\Delta H_c^{\ominus}[C_3H_6O_{(l)}] = -\ \textbf{1789.9 kJ mol}^{-1}$ (This is not the actual value due to state changes.)

Question 17	a)	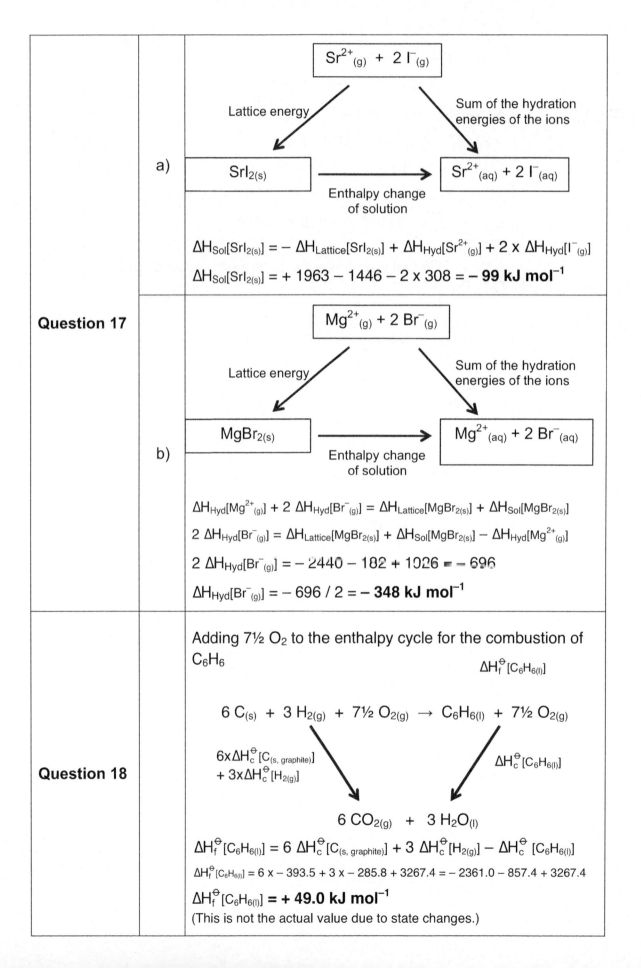 $Sr^{2+}_{(g)} + 2\,I^-_{(g)}$ Lattice energy Sum of the hydration energies of the ions $SrI_{2(s)}$ $\longrightarrow$ $Sr^{2+}_{(aq)} + 2\,I^-_{(aq)}$ Enthalpy change of solution $\Delta H_{Sol}[SrI_{2(s)}] = -\,\Delta H_{Lattice}[SrI_{2(s)}] + \Delta H_{Hyd}[Sr^{2+}_{(g)}] + 2 \times \Delta H_{Hyd}[I^-_{(g)}]$ $\Delta H_{Sol}[SrI_{2(s)}] = +\,1963 - 1446 - 2 \times 308 = \mathbf{-\,99\ kJ\ mol^{-1}}$
	b)	$Mg^{2+}_{(g)} + 2\,Br^-_{(g)}$ Lattice energy Sum of the hydration energies of the ions $MgBr_{2(s)}$ $\longrightarrow$ $Mg^{2+}_{(aq)} + 2\,Br^-_{(aq)}$ Enthalpy change of solution $\Delta H_{Hyd}[Mg^{2+}_{(g)}] + 2\,\Delta H_{Hyd}[Br^-_{(g)}] = \Delta H_{Lattice}[MgBr_{2(s)}] + \Delta H_{Sol}[MgBr_{2(s)}]$ $2\,\Delta H_{Hyd}[Br^-_{(g)}] = \Delta H_{Lattice}[MgBr_{2(s)}] + \Delta H_{Sol}[MgBr_{2(s)}] - \Delta H_{Hyd}[Mg^{2+}_{(g)}]$ $2\,\Delta H_{Hyd}[Br^-_{(g)}] = -\,2440 - 182 + 1026 = -\,696$ $\Delta H_{Hyd}[Br^-_{(g)}] = -\,696\,/\,2 = \mathbf{-\,348\ kJ\ mol^{-1}}$
Question 18		Adding 7½ O_2 to the enthalpy cycle for the combustion of C_6H_6 $\Delta H^{\ominus}_f[C_6H_{6(l)}]$ $6\,C_{(s)} + 3\,H_{2(g)} + 7½\,O_{2(g)} \rightarrow C_6H_{6(l)} + 7½\,O_{2(g)}$ $6 \times \Delta H^{\ominus}_c[C_{(s,\ graphite)}]$ + $3 \times \Delta H^{\ominus}_c[H_{2(g)}]$ $\Delta H^{\ominus}_c[C_6H_{6(l)}]$ $6\,CO_{2(g)} + 3\,H_2O_{(l)}$ $\Delta H^{\ominus}_f[C_6H_{6(l)}] = 6\,\Delta H^{\ominus}_c[C_{(s,\ graphite)}] + 3\,\Delta H^{\ominus}_c[H_{2(g)}] - \Delta H^{\ominus}_c[C_6H_{6(l)}]$ $\Delta H^{\ominus}_f[C_6H_{6(l)}] = 6 \times -393.5 + 3 \times -285.8 + 3267.4 = -2361.0 - 857.4 + 3267.4$ $\Delta H^{\ominus}_f[C_6H_{6(l)}] = \mathbf{+\,49.0\ kJ\ mol^{-1}}$ (This is not the actual value due to state changes.)

Question 19	a)	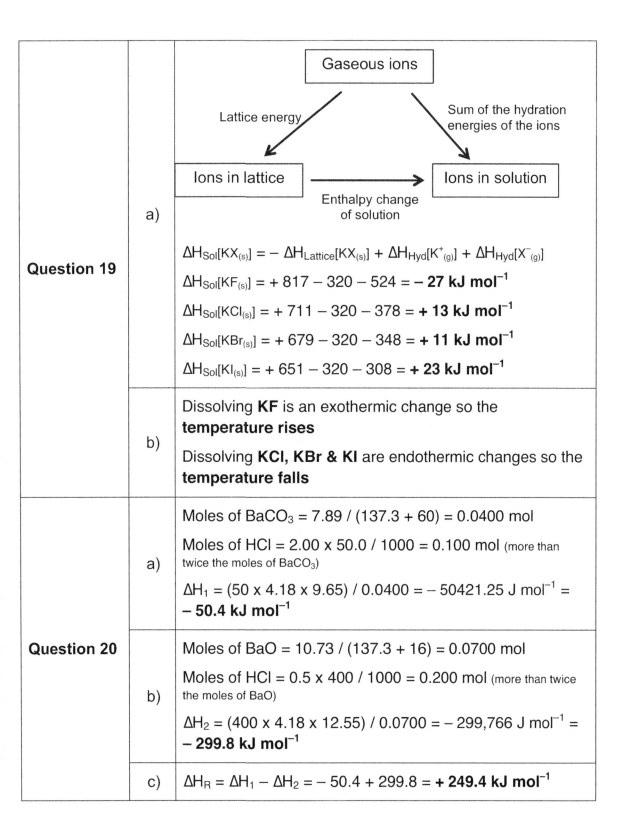 $\Delta H_{Sol}[KX_{(s)}] = - \Delta H_{Lattice}[KX_{(s)}] + \Delta H_{Hyd}[K^+_{(g)}] + \Delta H_{Hyd}[X^-_{(g)}]$ $\Delta H_{Sol}[KF_{(s)}] = + 817 - 320 - 524 = - \textbf{27 kJ mol}^{-1}$ $\Delta H_{Sol}[KCl_{(s)}] = + 711 - 320 - 378 = + \textbf{13 kJ mol}^{-1}$ $\Delta H_{Sol}[KBr_{(s)}] = + 679 - 320 - 348 = + \textbf{11 kJ mol}^{-1}$ $\Delta H_{Sol}[KI_{(s)}] = + 651 - 320 - 308 = + \textbf{23 kJ mol}^{-1}$
	b)	Dissolving **KF** is an exothermic change so the **temperature rises** Dissolving **KCl, KBr & KI** are endothermic changes so the **temperature falls**
Question 20	a)	Moles of $BaCO_3$ = 7.89 / (137.3 + 60) = 0.0400 mol Moles of HCl = 2.00 x 50.0 / 1000 = 0.100 mol (more than twice the moles of $BaCO_3$) ΔH_1 = (50 x 4.18 x 9.65) / 0.0400 = – 50421.25 J mol^{-1} = **– 50.4 kJ mol^{-1}**
	b)	Moles of BaO = 10.73 / (137.3 + 16) = 0.0700 mol Moles of HCl = 0.5 x 400 / 1000 = 0.200 mol (more than twice the moles of BaO) ΔH_2 = (400 x 4.18 x 12.55) / 0.0700 = – 299,766 J mol^{-1} = **– 299.8 kJ mol^{-1}**
	c)	$\Delta H_R = \Delta H_1 - \Delta H_2 = - 50.4 + 299.8 = + \textbf{249.4 kJ mol}^{-1}$

Question 21		*Creation of the gaseous ions:* $+89.2 + 419 + 111.9 - 324.6 = + 295.5$ kJ mol^{-1} *Lattice energy:* $- 295.5 - 393.8 = 689.3 =$ **689 kJ mol^{-1} to 3 s.f.**
Question 22		*Creation of the gaseous ions:* $2(+159.4 + 520) + 249.2 - 141.1 + 798 = + 2264.9$ kJ mol^{-1} *Lattice energy:* $- 2264.9 - 597.9 = 2862.8 =$ **2860 kJ mol^{-1} to 3 s.f.**
Question 23		*Creation of the gaseous ions:* $+178.2 + 590 + 1145 + 2(+106.8 - 295.4) = + 1536$ kJ mol^{-1} $\Delta H_{Lattice} = - 1536 - 533.5 = - 2069.5$ $= -$ **2070 kJ mol^{-1} to 3 s.f.**
Question 24		*Creation of the gaseous ions:* $2(+326.4 + 578 + 1817 + 2745) + 3(+249.2 - 141.1 + 798)$ $= 10932.8 + 2718.3 = + 13651.1$ kJ mol^{-1} $\Delta H_{Lattice} = - 13651.1 - 1675.7 = - 15326.8$ $= -$ **15300 kJ mol^{-1} to 3 s.f.**
Question 25		*Creation of the gaseous ions:* $(\Delta H^{\ominus}_{at}[Ga_{(s)}] + 579 + 1979 + 2963) + 3 \times (121.7 - 348.8)$ $= \Delta H^{\ominus}_{at}[Ga_{(s)}] + 4839.7$ kJ mol^{-1} $\Delta H_{Lattice} = - 5641 = - \Delta H^{\ominus}_{at}[Ga_{(s)}] - 4839.7 - 524.7$ $\Delta H^{\ominus}_{at}[Ga_{(s)}] = - 4839.7 - 524.7 + 5641 = + 276.6$ $= +$ **277 kJ mol^{-1}**
Question 26		*Creation of the gaseous ions:* $+ 147.7 + 278.8 + 738 + 1451 - 200.4 + \Delta H_{aff}[S^{-}_{(g)}]$ $= \Delta H_{aff}[S^{-}_{(g)}] + 2415.1$ kJ mol^{-1} $\Delta H_{Lattice} = - 3401 = - \Delta H_{aff}[S^{-}_{(g)}] - 2415.1 - 346.0$ $\Delta H_{aff}[S^{-}_{(g)}] = - 2415.1 - 346.0 + 3401 = + 639.9$ $= +$ **640 kJ mol^{-1} to 3 s.f.**
Question 27		*Creation of the gaseous ions:* $2(326.4 + 578 + 1817 + 2745) + 3(227.1 - 195.0 + 301)$ $= 10932.8 + 999.3 = + 11932.1$ kJ mol^{-1} $\Delta H^{\ominus}_{f}[Al_2O_{3(s)}] = + 11932.1 - 12499 = - 566.9$ $= -$ **567 kJ mol^{-1} to 3 s.f.**

Examination Style Questions

Question 1	a)	$Q = 500.0 \times 4.18 \times 26.2 = 54{,}758$ J **(1)** $\Delta H_c^{\ominus} = 54{,}758 / 0.01 = 5{,}475{,}800$ J mol^{-1} **(1)** **$\Delta H_c^{\ominus} = -5{,}475$ kJ mol^{-1} to 3 s.f. (1)**
	b)	Incomplete combustion **(1)** Not all heat captured by the water **(1)**
Question 2	a)	$Q = 255.0 \times 4.18 \times 0.86 = 916.674$ J **(1)** $\Delta H_{solution}^{\ominus} = 916.674 / 0.0550 = 16{,}666.8$ J mol^{-1} **(1)** **$\Delta H_{solution}^{\ominus} = +17$ kJ mol^{-1} to 2 s.f. (1)**
	b)	 Both gaseous ions correct **(1)** Both aqueous ions correct **(1)**
	c)	Sum of hydration energies $= \Delta H_{Lattice} + \Delta H_{solution}^{\ominus}$ $= -1755 + 17 = -1738$ $-1738 = 2 \times -524 + \Delta H_{Hydration}[M^{2+}]$ **(1)** $\Delta H_{Hydration}[M^{2+}] = -1738 + 1048$ **(1)** **$= -690$ kJ mol^{-1} to 2 s.f. (1)**
Question 3	a)	Elements box: $Sr_{(s)} + C_{(s,\ graphite)} + 1\tfrac{1}{2} O_{2(g)}$ **(1)** $\Delta H_R = -\Delta H_f^{\ominus}[SrCO_{3(s)}] + \Delta H_f^{\ominus}[SrO_{(s)}] + \Delta H_f^{\ominus}[CO_{2(g)}]$ $\Delta H_R = +1221.1 - 592.0 - 393.5$ **(1)** **$= +235.6$ kJ mol^{-1} to 4 s.f. (1)**
	b)	The reaction needs to overcome the activation energy **(1)**
	c)	Direct heating will mask the exchange of energy with the surroundings **(1)**

Question 4	a)	Orange gas colour fades to colourless **(1)**
	b)	*Long method:* Break: $4(C - H) + 1(Br - Br) = 4 \times 435 + 193$ $= + 1933$ kJ mol^{-1} **(1)** Make: $3(C - H) + 1(C - Br) + 1(H - Br) = 3 \times 435 + 290 + 366$ $= - 1961$ kJ mol^{-1} **(1)** Overall: $+ 1933 - 1961 = - \textbf{28 kJ mol}^{-1}$ **(1)** *Short method:* Break: $1(C - H) + 1(Br - Br) = 435 + 193$ $= + 628$ kJ mol^{-1} **(1)** Make: $1(C - Br) + 1(H - Br) = 290 + 366$ $= - 656$ kJ mol^{-1} **(1)** Overall: $+ 628 - 656 = - \textbf{28 kJ mol}^{-1}$ **(1)**
	c)	Free radical substitution **(1)**
	d)	(Homolytically) splits the Br_2 molecule to form 2 bromine atoms / bromine free radicals **(1)**
Question 5	a)	$Mg^{+}_{(g)} \rightarrow Mg^{2+}_{(g)} + e^{-}$ **(1)**
	b)	12 protons attracting only 11 electrons means each is more tightly held **(1)**
	c)	Top left box: $Mg^{2+}_{(g)} + 2 I_{(g)}$ **(1)** Bottom left box: $\Delta H^{\ominus}_{at} [Mg_{(s)}]$ **(1)** Right hand box: $\Delta H_{Lattice}$ or $\Delta_{lattice}H$ **(1)**
	d)	*Forming gaseous ions:* $+147.7 + 2189 + 2(106.8 - 295.4) = + 1959.5$ kJ mol^{-1} **(1)** Lattice energy $= - 1959.5 - 364.0 = - 2323.5$ **(1)** Lattice energy $= - \textbf{2320 kJ mol}^{-1}$ **to 3 s.f. (1)**

	e)	(i) Percentage difference $= 100 \times (2320 - 1944) / 1944$ **(1)**
		     $= \textbf{19.3 \%}$ **(1)**
		
		(ii) The iodide ion is large and singly charged (making it soft) **(1)**
		
		     The Mg ion is small and double positive charge (making it hard) **(1)**
		
		     The iodide ion is distorted towards some covalency by the Mg^{2+} **(1)**

Question 6	a)	Reaction is 1 : 2 for sulfuric acid : sodium hydroxide **(1)** Moles of H_2SO_4 = 2.00 x 20.0 / 1000 = 0.0400 mol ⎤ Moles of NaOH = 2.00 x 40.0 / 1000 = 0.0800 mol ⎦ **(1)** (twice moles of H_2SO_4)
	b)	Expt 1: (1:1 reaction) Moles of HCl and NaOH = 1.00 x 100.0 / 1000 = 0.100 mol **(1)** $\Delta H^{\ominus}_{neut}$ = (200.0 x 4.18 x 6.9) / 0.1 = 57,684 J mol^{-1} **= − 58 kJ mol^{-1} to 2 s.f. (1)** Expt 2: (1:1 reaction) Moles of HNO_3 and KOH = 2.00 x 40.0 / 1000 = 0.08 mol **(1)** $\Delta H^{\ominus}_{neut}$ = (80.0 x 4.18 x 13.9) / 0.08 = 58,102 J mol^{-1} **= − 58.1 kJ mol^{-1} to 3 s.f. (1)** Expt 3: (1:2 reaction) Moles of H_2SO_4 = 0.0400 mol **(1)** $\Delta H^{\ominus}_{neut}$ = (60.0 x 4.18 x 18.4) / 0.0400 = 115,368 J mol^{-1} **= − 115 kJ mol^{-1} to 3 s.f. (1)**
	c)	Expt 1 & Expt 2 have the same value as they both form 1 mole of water from a strong acid and strong alkali. **(1)** Expt 3 forms 2 moles of water so the value is approximately twice the magnitude of the other two experiments. **(1)**

Question 7	a)	$Cu_{(s)} + 2 Ag^+_{(aq)} \rightarrow Cu^{2+}_{(aq)} + 2Ag_{(s)}$ Correct species **(1)** Correct balancing and state symbols **(1)**
	b)	Moles of Cu = 1.00 / 63.5 = 0.01575 moles $\Big]$ **(1)** Moles Ag$^+$ = 0.100 x 200.0 / 1000 = 0.0200 moles 0.0200 moles of Ag$^+$ would need 0.0100 mol Cu. There is more than this. **(1)**
	c)	Q = 200.0 x 4.18 x 0.26 = 217.36 J **(1)** ΔH_R = 217.36 / 0.0100 = 21.736 kJ mol^{-1} **= − 22 kJ mol^{-1} to 2 s.f. (1)**
	d)	Increase the concentration of the silver nitrate and amount of copper powder used so that the uncertainty in the temperature rise decreases in magnitude. **(1)**

Question 8	a)	Endothermic **(1)**
	b)	$CaO_{(s)} + 2\,HCl_{(aq)} \rightarrow CaCl_{2(aq)} + H_2O_{(l)}$ Correct species **(1)** Correct balancing and state symbols **(1)**
	c)	Moles of $CaCO_3$ = 2.50 / (40.1 + 60) = 0.024975 mol = moles of CaO **(1)** Q = 20.0 x 4.18 x 24.5 = 2048.2 J **(1)** ΔH_{R1} = 2048.2 / 0.024975 = 82,010 = **– 82.0 kJ mol^{-1} (1)**
	d)	$CaCO_{3(s)} + 2\,HCl_{(aq)} > CaCl_{2(aq)} + CO_{2(g)} + H_2O_{(l)}$ Correct species **(1)** Correct balancing and state symbols **(1)**
	e)	Moles of $CaCO_3$ = 2.75 / (40.1 + 60) = 0.0274725 mol **(1)** Q = 20.0 x 4.18 x 4.50 = 376.2 J **(1)** ΔH_{R2} = 376.2 / 0.0274725 = 13,694 = **– 13.7 kJ mol^{-1} (1)**
	f)	 2 HCl on both sides **(1)** Correct products at the bottom **(1)** Correct placement of ΔH_{dec}, ΔH_{R1} and ΔH_{R2} **(1)**
	g)	$\Delta H_{dec}[CaCO_3] = \Delta H_{R2} - \Delta H_{R1}$ **(1)** $\Delta H_{dec}[CaCO_3] = -\,13.7 +\,82.0 = +\,68.3$ kJ mol^{-1} **(1)**

Question 9	a)	*Propene* Break: $6(C-H) + 1(C-C) + 1(C=C) + 4.5(O=O)$ $= 6 \times 413 + 347 + 612 + 4.5 \times 498 =$ **+ 5678 kJ mol^{-1} (1)** Make: $6(C=O) + 6(O-H)$ $= 6 \times 805 + 6 \times 464 =$ **− 7614 kJ mol^{-1} (1)** Overall: $+5678 - 7614 =$ **− 1936 kJ mol^{-1} (1)** *Cyclopropane* Break: $6(C-H) + 3(C-C) + 4.5(O=O)$ $= 6 \times 413 + 3 \times 347 + 4.5 \times 498 =$ **+ 5760 kJ mol^{-1} (1)** Make: $6(C=O) + 6(O-H)$ $= 6 \times 805 + 6 \times 464 =$ **− 7614 kJ mol^{-1} (1)** Overall: $+5760 - 7614 =$ **− 1854 kJ mol^{-1} (1)**
	b)	Not breaking the same bonds **(1)** Environment of the bonds broken is different in each compound **(1)**
Question 10	a)	$\Delta T = 3.0$ (K) Answer should be to 1 d.p. **(1)**
	b)	Half the number of moles of each reactant in Expt 2 **and** 2.5 times the volume of water. **(1)** Energy released will be halved **and** $\div 2.5$ for the volume **(1)** Temperature rise will be 3.0 K $\times 0.5 / 2.5 =$ **0.6 K (1)**
	c)	Digital thermometer **OR** temperature probe attached to a logging device **(1)**
	d)	$Mg^{2+}_{(aq)} + CO_3^{2-}_{(aq)} \rightarrow MgCO_{3(s)}$ Correct species **(1)** Correct state symbols **(1)**
	e)	Reaction is 1:1 ratio Moles of each reactant $= 1.0 \times 20.0 / 1000 = 0.020$ mol **(1)** $\Delta H_{pptn} = 40.0 \times 4.18 \times 3.0 / 0.02$ **(1)** $= 25,080$ J mol$^{-1} =$ **− 25 kJ mol^{-1} to 2 s.f. (1)**

Question 11	a)	Fume cupboard / extractor hood **(1)** Carbon monoxide released **(1)**
	b)	The thermal energy used to decompose the $SrSO_4$ masks the thermal exchange with the surroundings. **(1)**
	c)	Enthalpy change of formation for any element in its standard state is zero. **(1)** **OR** Definition of enthalpy change of formation is the formation of a substance from its constituent elements in their standard states. Forming carbon involves no change. **(1)**
	d)	$\Delta H_R = + 1453.1 - 453.1 + 4 \times -110.5$ **(1)** $= + 558.0$ **kJ mol^{-1} to 4 s.f. (1)**

Question 12	a)	$C_4H_8 + 6 O_2 \rightarrow 4 CO_2 + 4 H_2O$ Correct species **(1)** Correct balancing and state symbols **(1)**
	b)	$$6 O_{2(g)} + 4 C_{(s)} + 4 H_{2(g)} \xrightarrow{\Delta H_f^{\ominus}[C_4H_{8(g)}]} C_4H_{8(g)} + 6 O_{2(g)}$$ $4 \times \Delta H_f^{\ominus}[CO_{2(g)}] + 4 \times \Delta H_f^{\ominus}[H_2O_{(l)}]$ $\Delta H_c^{\ominus}[C_4H_{8(g)}]$ $$4 CO_{2(g)} + 4 H_2O_{(l)}$$ Adding $6 O_{2(g)}$ **(1)** Adding $4 CO_{2(g)} + 4 H_2O_{(l)}$ **(1)** Adding $4 \times \Delta H_f^{\ominus}[CO_{2(g)}] + 4 \times \Delta H_f^{\ominus}[H_2O_{(l)}]$ ⎤ Adding $\Delta H_c^{\ominus}[C_4H_{8(g)}]$ ⎦ **(1)** $\Delta H_f^{\ominus}[C_4H_{8(g)}] = 4 \times \Delta H_f^{\ominus}[CO_{2(g)}] + 4 \times \Delta H_f^{\ominus}[H_2O_{(l)}] - \Delta H_c^{\ominus}[C_4H_{8(g)}]$ $\Delta H_f^{\ominus}[C_4H_{8(g)}] = 4 \times -393.5 + 4 \times -285.8 + 2716.8$ **(1)** $\Delta H_f^{\ominus}[C_4H_{8(g)}] = -0.4 \text{ kJ mol}^{-1}$ **(1)**
	c)	$C_4H_8 + 6 O_2 \rightarrow 4 CO_2 + 4 H_2O$ But-1-ene is $CH_3CH_2CH=CH_2$ Break: $8(C-H) + 2(C-C) + 1(C=C) + 6(O=O)$ $= 8 \times 413 + 2 \times 347 + 612 + 6 \times 498 = +7598 \text{ kJ mol}^{-1}$ **(1)** Make: $8 \times 805 + 8 \times 464 = -10{,}152 \text{ kJ mol}^{-1}$ **(1)** Overall: $+7598 - 10152 = -2554 \text{ kJ mol}^{-1}$ **(1)**
	d)	Bond enthalpies are mean values not specific to individual compounds **(1)** Bond enthalpies are for substances in the gaseous state. (Water is a liquid in the equation.) **(1)**

Question 13	a)	The enthalpy change under standard conditions to form 1 mole of separate atoms **(1)**
		of an element in the gaseous state **(1)**
		from the element in its standard state. **(1)**
	b)	$$2 \text{ As}_{(s)} \quad + \quad 3 \text{ F}_{2(g)} \quad \rightarrow \quad 2 \text{ AsF}_{3(g)}$$ $$- 1841.2 \text{ kJ mol}^{-1}$$ $2 \times \Delta H^{\ominus}_{at}[\text{As}_{(s)}] +$ $6 \times \Delta H^{\ominus}_{at}[\tfrac{1}{2} \text{ F}_{2(g)}]$ $\qquad\qquad 6(\text{As} - \text{F})$ $$2 \text{ As}_{(g)} \quad + \quad 6 \text{ F}_{(g)}$$ $6(\text{As} - \text{F}) = (2 \times \Delta H^{\ominus}_{at}[\text{As}_{(g)}] + 6 \times \Delta H^{\ominus}_{at}[\text{F}_{(g)}]) + 1841.2$ **OR** Hess Cycle **(1)** $6(\text{As} - \text{F}) = (2 \times 302.5 + 6 \times 79.0) + 1841.2$ **(1)** $6(\text{As} - \text{F}) = 1079 + 1841.2$ $(\text{As} - \text{F}) = 2920.2 / 6 = + 486.7 = \mathbf{+ 487 \text{ kJ mol}^{-1}}$ **(1)**

Question 14	a)	Ge has an atomic number of 32 $1s^2\ 2s^2\ 2p^6\ 3s^2\ 3p^6\ 3d^{10}\ 4s^2\ 4p^2$ **(1)**
	b)	The P block **(1)**
	c)	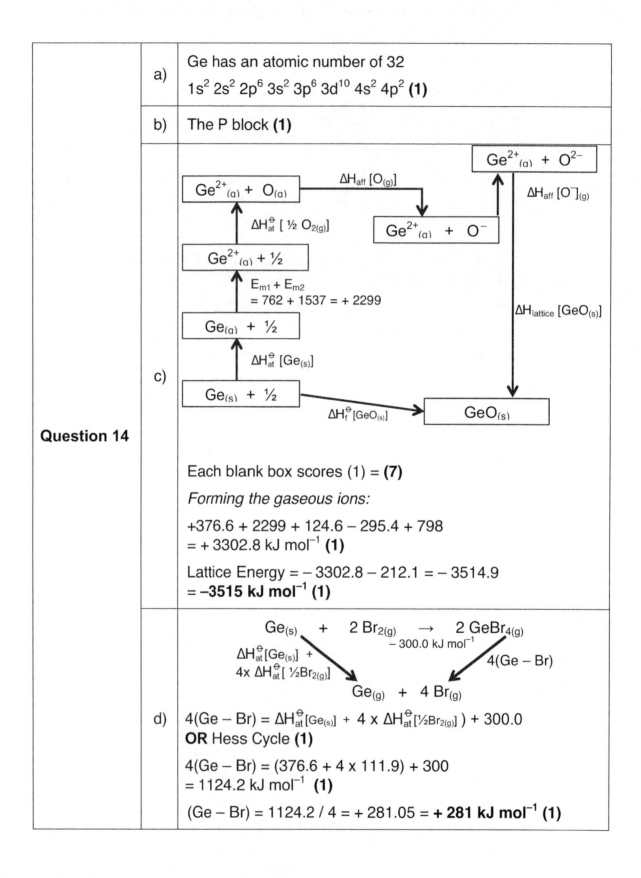 Each blank box scores (1) = **(7)** *Forming the gaseous ions:* +376.6 + 2299 + 124.6 − 295.4 + 798 = + 3302.8 kJ mol^{-1} **(1)** Lattice Energy = − 3302.8 − 212.1 = − 3514.9 **= −3515 kJ mol^{-1} (1)**
	d)	$4(Ge - Br) = \Delta H^{\ominus}_{at}[Ge_{(s)}] + 4 \times \Delta H^{\ominus}_{at}[\frac{1}{2}Br_{2(g)}]) + 300.0$ **OR** Hess Cycle **(1)** $4(Ge - Br) = (376.6 + 4 \times 111.9) + 300$ $= 1124.2$ kJ mol^{-1} **(1)** $(Ge - Br) = 1124.2 / 4 = + 281.05 =$ **+ 281 kJ mol^{-1} (1)**

Question 15	a)	*Procedure 1:* $Q = 50.0 \times 4.18 \times (55.8 - 18.5) = 7795.7$ J **(1)** Moles of Mg = 1.05 / 24.3 = 0.04321 mol Moles HCl = 2.00 × 50 / 1000 = 0.100 mol }**(1)** Equation is Mg : HCl in a ratio of 1 : 2 so moles of HCl needed = 0.08642 meaning that the HCl is in excess. **(1)** $\Delta H_{R1} = 7795.7 / 0.04321 = 180{,}414$ J mol^{-1} $= -$ **180 kJ mol^{-1} to 3 s.f. (1)** Procedure 2: $Q = 60.0 \times 4.18 \times (25.0 - 20.2) = 1203.84$ J **(1)** Moles of MgO = 2.05 / (24.3 + 16) = 0.0508685 mol Moles of HCl = 2.00 × 60 / 1000 = 0.120 mol }**(1)** Equation is MgO : HCl in a ratio of 1 : 2 so moles of HCl needed is 0.10174 meaning that the HCl is in excess. **(1)** $\Delta H_{R2} = 1203.84 / 0.0508685 = 23{,}666$ J mol^{-1} $= -$ **23.7 kJ mol^{-1} to 3 s.f. (1)**
	b)	$2\,HCl_{(aq)} + Mg_{(s)} + \tfrac{1}{2}\,O_{2(g)} \rightarrow MgO_{(s)} + 2\,HCl_{(aq)}$ **(1)** $MgCl_{2(aq)} + H_{2(g)} + \tfrac{1}{2}\,O_{2(g)} \rightarrow MgCl_{2(aq)} + H_2O_{(l)}$ **(1)**
	c)	$\Delta H_f^{\ominus}[MgO_{(s)}] = \Delta H_{R1} + \Delta H_f^{\ominus}[H_2O_{(l)}] - \Delta H_{R2}$ **(1)** $\Delta H_f^{\ominus}[MgO_{(s)}] = -180 - 285.8 + 23.7 = -442.1$ kJ mol^{-1} **(1)** $\Delta H_f^{\ominus}[MgO_{(s)}] = -$ **442 kJ mol^{-1} to 3 s.f. (1)**
	d)	Percentage difference = 100 × (601.7 − 442) / 601.7 = **26.5 % (1)**

Question 16	a)	$4\frac{1}{2}\,O_{2(g)} + 2\,C_{(s)} + 3\,H_{2(g)} + S_{(s)} \rightarrow C_2H_5SH_{(l)} + 4\frac{1}{2}\,O_{2(g)}$ ΔH_1 $\boxed{\Delta H_c^{\ominus}[C_2H_5SH_{(l)}]}$ $2\,CO_{2(g)} + 3\,H_2O_{(l)} + SO_{2(g)}$ $4\frac{1}{2}\,O_{2(g)}$ on both sides of the equation **(1)** $\Delta H_c^{\ominus}[C_2H_5SH_{(l)}]$ added to box **(1)**
	b)	$\Delta H_f^{\ominus}[CO_{2(g)}]$ **(1)** $\Delta H_f^{\ominus}[H_2O_{(l)}]$ **(1)** $\Delta H_f^{\ominus}[SO_{2(g)}]$ **(1)**
	c)	$2 \times \Delta H_f^{\ominus}[CO_{2(g)}] + 3 \times \Delta H_f^{\ominus}[H_2O_{(l)}] + \Delta H_f^{\ominus}[SO_{2(g)}] = \Delta H_f^{\ominus}[C_2H_5SH_{(l)}] + \Delta H_c^{\ominus}[C_2H_5SH_{(l)}]$ **(1)** $-\ 2 \times 393.5 - 3 \times 285.8 + \Delta H_f^{\ominus}[SO_{2(g)}] = -73.7 - 2173.2$ **(1)** $\Delta H_f^{\ominus}[SO_{2(g)}] = -73.7 - 2173.2 + 787.0 + 857.4$ $= -\mathbf{602.5\ kJ\ mol^{-1}}$ **(1)** (Note: the actual value is -296.8 kJ mol^{-1}. There is a simplification in here with the sulfur.)

Question 17	a)

Double bond **(1)**

Unpaired electron on the nitrogen atom **(1)**

Double bond and single dative covalent bond **(1)**

Unpaired electon on the nitrogen atom **(1)** |
| | b) | $NO_{(g)} + \frac{1}{2} O_{2(g)} \rightarrow NO_{2(g)}$ **(1)**
(Doubled balancing is allowed) |
| | c) | *Part (i)*

Break: $1(N = O) + \frac{1}{2}(O = O) = 587 + \frac{1}{2} \times 498 = + 836$ kJ mol^{-1} **(1)**

Make: $1(N = O) + 1(N - O) = 587 + 214 = - 801$ kJ mol^{-1} **(1)**

Overall: $+ 836 - 801 = $ **+ 35 kJ mol^{-1} (1)**

(The doubled balancing gives an answer of $+ 70$ kJ mol^{-1})

Part (ii)

$\Delta H_f^{\ominus} = + 33.2 - 90.2 = $ **– 57.0 kJ mol^{-1} (1)**

(The doubled balancing gives an answer of $- 114$ kJ mol^{-1})

Part (iii)

Bonding is different to the dot and cross diagram **(1)**

Bonding is delocalised which changes the bond energy **(1)** |
| | d) | *Break:* $1(N \equiv N) + 1(O = O) = 945 + 498 = + 1443$ kJ mol^{-1} **(1)**

Make: $2(N = O) = 2E$

Overall: $= 2 \times \Delta H_f^{\ominus}[NO_{(g)}] = 2 \times +90.2 = + 180.4$ kJ mol^{-1} **(1)**

$+ 180.4 = +1443 - 2E$

$E = (1443 - 180.4) / 2 = + 631.3 = $ **+631 kJ mol^{-1} (1)** |
| | e) | At lower temperatures NO will react with O_2 due to the exothermic change of ΔH_{R2} **(1)**

At higher temperatures the more endothermic ΔH_{R2} can take place. **(1)**

(The real reason lies with the entropy changes for the reaction which is contained in Book 5.) |

Question 18	a)	With the exothermic value for the reaction with carbon dioxide and water **(1)** $NaHCO_3$ is more thermally stable than Na_2CO_3 **(1)**
	b)	The formation of 1 mole of a substance under standard conditions **(1)** From its constituent elements in their standard states **(1)**
	c)	$-91.0 = -(\Delta H_f^{\ominus}[Na_2CO_{3(s)}] + \Delta H_f^{\ominus}[CO_{2(g)}] + \Delta H_f^{\ominus}[H_2O_{(l)}] + 2\ \Delta H_f^{\ominus}[NaHCO_{3(s)}]$ $-91.0 = +1131 + 394 + 286 + 2\ \Delta H_f^{\ominus}[NaHCO_{3(s)}]$ **(1)** $-91.0 = +1811 + 2\ \Delta H_f^{\ominus}[NaHCO_{3(s)}]$ $2\ \Delta H_f^{\ominus}[NaHCO_{3(s)}] = -91.0 - 1811 = -1902\ kJ\ mol^{-1}$ **(1)** $\Delta H_f^{\ominus}[NaHCO_{3(s)}] = -1902 / 2 =$ **$-951\ kJ\ mol^{-1}$ to 3 s.f. (1)**
Question 19	a)	$M_r[UO_2(NO_3)_2.6H_2O] = 238 + 32 + 2 \times 62 + 6 \times 18 = 502$ **(1)** % U by mass $= 100 \times 238 / 502 =$ **47.4 % (1)**
	b)	Uranium: **neither** (+6 on both sides) Hydrogen: **neither** (+1 on both sides) $\Big\}$ **(1)** Oxygen: **oxidised** (from –2 to 0) Nitrogen: **reduced** (from +5 to +4) $\Big\}$ **(1)**
	c)	$\Delta H_{dec} = -1264 \times 2 + -285.8 \times 6 + 33.1 \times 4 + 2 \times 3198$ **(1)** $\Delta H_{dec} = -2528 + -1714.8 + 132.4 + 6396 = +2285.6\ kJ\ mol^{-1}$ (1) $\Delta H_{dec} =$ **$+2290\ kJ\ mol^{-1}$ (1)** to 3 s.f.

Question 20	a)	They are both elements in their standard states. **(1)**
	b)	Less (due to the reaction being exothermic) **(1)**
	c)	$\Delta H_R = +319.7 - 443.5$ **(1)** $\Delta H_R = -123.8$ **(1)** $kJ\ mol^{-1}$ **(1)**
	d)	*Break:* $1(Cl-Cl) = +234\ kJ\ mol^{-1}$ *Make:* $2(P-Cl) = 2 \times 328 = -656\ kJ\ mol^{-1}$ } **(1)** *Overall:* $+234 - 656 = -422\ kJ\ mol^{-1}$ **(1)**
	e)	*In either order:* Bond energies are mean values and are not specific to particular compounds **(1)** Both PCl_3 and PCl_5 are not in the gaseous state **(1)**
	f)	Part (i) *Left box:* $+446$ **(1)** *Right box:* $4 \times -249 = -996$ **(1)** Part (ii) $\Delta H_R = -446 - 996$ **(1)** $\Delta H_R = -1442\ kJ\ mol^{-1}$ **(1)** Part (iii) *Break:* $6(P-P) + 6(Cl-Cl) = 6E + 6 \times 243 = 6E + 1458\ kJ\ mol^{-1}$ *Make:* $12(P-Cl) = 12 \times 328 = -3936\ kJ\ mol^{-1}$ } **(1)** Overall: $-1442 = 6E + 1458 - 3936 = 6E - 2478$ $E = (-1442 + 2478) / 6$ **(1)** $E(P-P) = +172.67 = +173\ kJ\ mol^{-1}$ **(1)**

Question 21	a)	To heat and cook requires energy to be released to the surroundings which is the definition of an exothermic change. **(1)**
	b)	*Break:* $2(C - C) + 8(C - H) + 5(O = O)$ $694 + = 2 \times 347 + 8 \times 413 + 5 \times 498 = 694 + 3304 + 2490$ $= + 6488$ kJ mol^{-1} **(1)** *Make:* $6((C = O) + 8(O - H)$ $= 6 \times 805 + 8 \times 464 = 4830 + 3712 = - 8542$ kJ mol^{-1} **(1)** Overall: $6488 - 8542 = $ **− 2054 kJ mol^{-1} (1)**
	c)	Bond energies are mean values rather than exact values for specific molecules **(1)**
	d)	Percentage difference $= 100 \times (2219 - 2054) / 2219$ $= $ **7.44 % (1)**
Question 22	a)	*Break:* $2(C \equiv N) + 1(C - C) + 1(O = O)$ $694 + = 2 \times 887 + 347 + 498 = 1774 + 347 + 498 = + 2619$ kJ mol^{-1} **(1)** *Make:* $2(C \equiv O) + 1(N \equiv N)$ $= 2 \times 1077 + 945 = 2154 + 945 = - 3099$ kJ mol^{-1} **(1)** Overall: $2619 - 3099 = $ **− 480 kJ mol^{-1} (1)**
	b)	Equation: $2 C_{(s, \text{graphite})} + N_{2(g)} \rightarrow (CN)_{2(g)}$ *Break.* $1(N = N) = +945$ kJ mol^{-1} **(1)** *Make:* $2(C \equiv N) + 1(C - C) = 2 \times 887 + 347 = - 2121$ kJ mol^{-1} **(1)** Overall: $+945 - 2121 = - 1176$ kJ mol^{-1} **(1)**
	c)	Bond energy calculations are for gaseous atoms and molecules. The carbon is a solid. (The $C_{(s)}$ would need to be atomised which is a large endothermic change). **(1)** [Including $2 \times \Delta H^{\ominus}_{at}[C_{s, \text{graphite}}]$] gives a value of $+ 257.4$ kJ mol^{-1}]
	d)	*Break:* $1(C - C) + 2(C = O) + 2(C - N) + 4(N - H)$ $= 347 + 2 \times 805 + 2 \times 286 + 4 \times 391 = 347 + 1610 + 572 + 1564$ $= +4093$ kJ mol^{-1} **(1)** *Make:* $2(C \equiv N) + 1(C - C) + 4(H - O)$ $= 2 \times 887 + 347 + 4 \times 464 = - 3977$ kJ mol^{-1} **(1)** Overall: $+4093 - 3977 = + 116$ kJ mol^{-1} **(1)**
	e)	Bond energies are mean values not exact values for specific molecules **(1)**

Question 23	a)	Enthalpy change of formation is defined as the formation of elements under standard conditions in their standard states. Oxygen as O_2 is an element in its standard state. **(1)**
	b)	Less **(1)** <small>All combustion reactions are exothermic where reactants lose energy to form the products.</small>
	c)	*Right box:* $2 \Delta H_f^\ominus[CO_{2(g)}] + 2 \Delta H_f^\ominus[H_2O_{(l)}]$ **(1)** *Bottom box:* $2 C_{(s, graphite)} + 2 H_{2(g)} + 3 O_{2(g)}$ **(1)**
	d)	$\Delta H_R = -52.2 - 2\times393.5 - 2\times285.8$ **(1)** $\Delta H_R = -$ **1410.8 kJ mol^{-1} (1)**
Question 24	a)	$C_{(s, graphite)} + 2 H_{2(g)}$ Species **(1)**　　　State symbols **(1)**
	b)	$2 O_{2(g)} + C_{(s, graphite)} + 2 H_{2(g)} \rightarrow CH_{4(g)} + 2 O_{2(g)}$ $-393.5 - 2\times285.8$　　　　　　　　　-890.3 $= -965.1$ 　　　　　　$CO_{2(g)} + 2 H_2O_{(l)}$ Elements in full at the bottom of Hess Cycle **(1)** Oxygen added to cycle on both sides **AND** correct numbers on arrows **(1)** $\Delta H_f^\ominus[CH_{4(g)}] = -965.1 + 890.3 = -74.8$ kJ mol^{-1} **(1)**
	c)	$\Delta H_R = \Delta H_f^\ominus[C_2H_{6(g)}] - 2 \Delta H_f^\ominus[CH_{4(g)}]$ **(1)** $\Delta H_R = -84.7 + 2\times74.8 = +$ **64.9 kJ mol^{-1} (1)**
Question 25	a)	$\Delta H_R = +704.2 + 6\times285.8 - 2691.6$ **(1)** $\Delta H_R = 272.6$ kJ mol^{-1} **(1)** $\Delta H_R = -$ **272.6 kJ mol^{-1} to 4 s.f. (1)**
	b)	The $AlCl_3$ will get hotter as the hydration is exothermic. **(1)**
	c)	The use of a heat source will mask the number of joules exchanged by the reaction.　**(1)**
	d)	Endothermic **(1)**
	e)	$\Delta H_{dec} = +2691.6 - 1287.4 - 3\times285.8 - 3\times92.3$ **(1)** $\Delta H_{dec} = +269.9$ **(1)** $\Delta H_{dec} = +$ **270 kJ mol^{-1} to 3 s.f. (1)**

Question 26	a)	Formula of ethyl pentanoate = $CH_3CH_2CH_2CH_2CO_2CH_2CH_3$ = $C_7H_{14}O_2$ **(1)** Mass of C = 4.857 x 12 / 44 = 1.325 g of C Mass of H = 1.987 x 2 / 18 = 0.221 g of H $\left.\right\}$ **(1)** Mass of O = 2.050 – 1.325 – 0.221 = 0.504 g of O Moles of each: C: 1.325 / 12 = 0.110 mol H: 0.221 / 1 = 0.221 mol $\left.\right\}$ **(1)** O: 0.504 / 16 = 0.0315 mol Divide by smallest: Ratio C : H : O = 3.5 : 7 : 1 = 7 : 14 : 2 as in molecular formula of ethyl pentanoate **(1)**
	b)	$\Delta H_R = -4.6 = +557.8 + 277.1 - 285.8 + \Delta H_f^{\ominus}[C_7H_{14}O_{2(s)}]$ **(1)** $\Delta H_f^{\ominus}[C_7H_{14}O_{2(s)}] = -4.6 - 557.8 - 277.1 + 285.8$ **(1)** $\Delta H_f^{\ominus}[C_7H_{14}O_{2(s)}] = \mathbf{-553.7\ kJ\ mol^{-1}}$ **(1)**
	c)	$9.5\ O_{2(g)} \rightarrow 7\ CO_{2(g)} + 7\ H_2O_{(l)}$ RHS balancing **(1)** LHS balancing **(1)**
	d)	$\Delta H_c^{\ominus}[C_7H_{14}O_{2(s)}] = +553.7 - 7 \times 393.5 + 7 \times 285.8$ **(1)** $\Delta H_c^{\uplus}[C_7H_{14}O_{2(s)}] = -4201.4\ kJ\ mol^{-1}$ **(1)** $\Delta H_c^{\ominus}[C_7H_{14}O_{2(s)}] = \mathbf{-4201\ kJ\ mol^{-1}}$ **to 4 s.f. (1)**
	e)	*Biofuel:* A fuel formed from biomass. **(1)** *Drop in biofuel:* A fuel that can be used as a direct replacement in a mixture of fossil fuel and biofuel. **(1)** *Not the answer:* Conflict between growing food and growing biofuels. **(1)** Still release CO_2 **OR** use fossil fuels in manufacturing process / transport to points of sale **(1)**

Question 27	a)	Mass of cyclohexane burned = 1.80 g (Reject 1.8 g) Temperature change = 37.0 °C (Reject 37 °C) Both required for **(1)**
	b)	402 x 4.18 x 37.0 = 62,173.33 J **(1)**
	c)	Moles of cyclohexane = 1.80 / 84.0 = 0.02143 mol **(1)**
	d)	$\Delta H_c^\ominus$ = 62173.33 / 0.02143 = 2,901,229 J **(1)** $\Delta H_c^\ominus$ = **− 2900 kJ mol^{-1} to 3 s.f. (1)**
	e)	Percentage difference = 100 x (3920 − 2900) / 3920 = **26.0 % to 3 s.f. (1)**
	f)	

Equipment	Uncertainty	Times used	Value measured	Percentage uncertainty
Thermometer	± 0.05 °C	2	**37.0 °C**	0.27 %
500 cm^3 measuring cylinder	± 5 cm^3	1	400 cm^3	1.25 %
Balance	± 0.005 g	2	**1.80 g**	0.56 %
			Total Percentage Uncertainty =	**2.08 %**

Thermometer row all correct **(1)**

Measuring cylinder row correct **(1)**

Balance row correct **(1)**

Total percentage uncertainty correct **(1)**

	g)	A 2.08 % uncertainty on a value of − 2900 kJ mol^{-1} has: 0.0208 x 2900 = ± 60 kJ mol^{-1} Minimum value: **− 2960 kJ mol^{-1} (1)** Maximum value: **− 2840 kJ mol^{-1} (1)**
	h)	Incomplete combustion **(1)** Not all heat released is captured by the water **(1)** Equipment used heats up **(1)**
Question 28	a)	Moles of ethylamine = 387 / 24000 = 0.016125 mol **(1)** Q = 350 x 4.18 x (33.7 − 17.5) = 23,700.6 J **(1)** $\Delta H_c^\ominus$ = 23700.6 / 0.016125 = 1,469,805 J mol^{-1} **(1)** $\Delta H_c^\ominus$ = **− 1470 kJ mol^{-1} to 3 s.f. (1)**
	b)	Different bonding within the structures is being broken **(1)**
	c)	Incomplete combustion **OR** heat not captured by the water **(1)**

Question 29	a)	The enthalpy change on the formation of a substance from its constituent elements **(1)** Under standard conditions **(1)**
	b)	The enthalpy change of formation of any element in its standard state is defined as zero **(1)**
	c)	Elements: $2\ Mn_{(s)}\ +\ 2\ O_{2(g)}$ **(2)** 1 mark for the elements and balancing 1 mark is for the state symbols $\Delta H_R = 2 \times 385.2 - 2 \times 520.0$ **(1)** $= -269.6\ kJ\ mol^{-1}$ **(1)**
Question 30	a)	$C_5H_{11}OH_{(l)}\ +\ 7.5\ O_{2(g)}\ \rightarrow\ 5\ CO_{2(g)}\ +\ 6\ H_2O_{(l)}$ **(1)**
	b)	Mass burned = 1.40 g **(1)** (Reject 1.4 g)
	c)	$Q = 400.00 \times 4.18 \times 24.5 = 40{,}964\ J$ **(1)** Moles of pentan-1-ol = 1.40 / 88.0 = 0.01591 mol **(1)** $\Delta H_c^{\ominus}[C_5H_{11}OH_{(l)}] = 40964 / 0.01591 = 2{,}574{,}733\ J\ mol^{-1}$ **(1)** $\Delta H_c^{\ominus}[C_5H_{11}OH_{(l)}] = -\ 2570\ kJ\ mol^{-1}$ **to 3 s.f. (1)**
	d)	Percentage difference = 100 x (3329.0 – 2570) / 3329.0 = **22.8 % (1)**
	e)	Temperature rise: 100 x 0.1 / 24.5 = **0.408 % (1)** Burner mass change: 100 x 0.01 / 1.40 = **0.714 % (1)**
	f)	Total uncertainty = 0.408 + 0.714 + 0.0025 = 1.1245 % = **1.12 % to 3 s.f. (1)**
	g)	2570 x 1.12 / 100 = 28.784 $kJ\ mol^{-1}$ = 30 $kJ\ mol^{-1}$ $\Delta H_c^{\ominus}[C_5H_{11}OH_{(l)}] = -\ 2570 \pm 30\ kJ\ mol^{-1}$ **(1)** (30 (not 29) matches the level of accuracy of $\Delta H_c^{\ominus}$)
	h)	Burn more pentan-1-ol **(1)** Higher mass change which lowers the uncertainty in the burner mass change **(1)** More energy will be released raising the water temperature higher, reducing the temperature change uncertainty **(1)**

Question 31	a)	$$4.5\ O_{2(g)}\ +\ 3\ C_{(s,\ graphite)}\ +\ 3\ H_{2(g)}\ \xrightarrow{\Delta H_f^{\ominus}[C_3H_{6(g)}]}\ C_3H_{6(g)}\ +\ 4.5\ O_{2(g)}$$ $$3\ \Delta H_c^{\ominus}[C_{(s,\ graphite)}]\ +\ 3\ \Delta H_c^{\ominus}[H_{2(g)}]\searrow\quad\swarrow\Delta H_c^{\ominus}[C_3H_{6(g)}]$$ $$3\ CO_{2(g)}\ +\ 3\ H_2O_{(l)}$$ $\Delta H_f^{\ominus}[C_3H_{6(g)}] = 3\ \Delta H_c^{\ominus}[C_{(s,\ graphite)}] + 3\ \Delta H_c^{\ominus}[H_{2(g)}] - \Delta H_c^{\ominus}[C_3H_{6(g)}]$ $\Delta H_f^{\ominus}[C_3H_{6(g)}] = 3\ x - 393.5 + 3\ x - 285.8 + 2058$ Enthalpy cycle with $4.5\ O_{2(g)}$ and $3\ CO_{2(g)} + 3\ H_2O_{(l)}$ **(1)** All symbols **OR** numbers on the arrows **(1)** Calculation of $\Delta H_f^{\ominus}[C_3H_{6(g)}]$ as above **(1)** Value of $\Delta H_f^{\ominus}[C_3H_{6(g)}] = \mathbf{+\ 20.1\ kJ\ mol^{-1}}$ **(1)**
	b)	The molecules are isomers of each other **(1)** The permanent dipole is a different size causing a difference in the intermolecular bonding **(1)**
	c)	$\Delta H_{R,\text{1-bromo}} = -\ 20.1 + 36.4 - 116.4$ **(1)** $= -\ 100.1\ kJ\ mol^{-1}$ **(1)** $\Delta H_{R,\text{2-bromo}} = -\ 20.1 + 36.4 - 128.5$ **(1)** $= -\ 112.2\ kJ\ mol^{-1}$ **(1)**
	d)	(i) Breaking and making the same bonds in the same numbers **(1)** (ii) Bond energies depend on the surrounding bonds which are not identical between the two isomers **(1)**
Question 32	a)	*Break:* $5(C - C) + 7(C - O) + 5(O - H) + 7(C - H) + 6(O = O)$ $= 5x347 + 7x358 + 5x464 + 7x413 + 6x498$ **(1)** $= 1735 + 2506 + 2320 + 2891 + 2988 = +\ 12440\ kJ\ mol^{-1}$ **(1)** *Make:* $12(C = O) + 12(O - H)$ $= 12x805 + 12x464$ **(1)** $= 9660 + 5568 = -\ 15228\ kJ\ mol^{-1}$ **(1)** *Overall:* $\Delta H_c^{\ominus}[C_6H_{12}O_{6(s)}] = +\ 12440 - 15228 = \mathbf{-\ 2788\ kJ\ mol^{-1}}$ **(1)**
	b)	Bond energies are for the gasous state, glcose is a solid, water is a liquid. **(1)** Bond energies are mean values, not the same in all compounds. **(1)**

Question 33	a)	*Break:* $1(C - Br) + 1(H - C) = 285 + 435 = + 720 \text{ kJ mol}^{-1}$ **(1)** *Make:* $1(C - C) + 1(H - Br) = - (347 + E)$ **(1)** *Overall:* $\Delta H_R = - 10 = +720 - 347 - E$ **(1)** $E = 720 - 347 + 10 = \textbf{+ 383 kJ mol}^{-1}$ **(1)**
	b)	$$CH_2ClCH_2Cl_{(g)} \rightarrow CH_2 = CHCl_{(g)} + HCl_{(g)}$$ $\Delta H_f^{\ominus}[CH_2ClCH_2Cl_{(g)}] \qquad \Delta H_f^{\ominus}[CH_2=CHCl_{(g)}] + \Delta H_f^{\ominus}[HCl_{(g)}]$ $$2\ C_{(s,\ graphite)} + 2\ H_{2(g)} + Cl_{2(g)}$$ **Formation of $CH_2 = CHCl_{(g)}$** *Break:* $2\ \Delta H_{at}^{\ominus}[C_{(s,\ graphite)}] + 1\tfrac{1}{2}(H - H) + \tfrac{1}{2}(Cl - Cl)$ **(1)** $= 2\text{x}716.7 + 1.5\text{x}436 + \tfrac{1}{2}\text{x}243 = 1433.4 + 654 + 121.5$ $= + 2208.9 \text{ kJ mol}^{-1}$ **(1)** *Make:* $1(C = C) + 3(C - H) + 1(C - Cl)$ $= 347 + 3\text{x}413 + 346 = - 1932 \text{ kJ mol}^{-1}$ **(1)** *Overall:* $+ 2208.9 - 1932 = \textbf{+ 276.9 kJ mol}^{-1}$ **(1)**

Question 34	a)	$H_2SO_{4(aq)}$ + 2 $NaOH_{(aq)}$ → $Na_2SO_{4(aq)}$ + 2 $H_2O_{(l)}$ Correct formulae **(1)** Correct balancing **(1)**
	b)	Moles of NaOH = 0.500 x 240 / 1000 = 0.120 mol ⎤ Moles of H_2SO_4 = 0.800 x 75.0 / 1000 = 0.0600 mol ⎦ **(1)** Reaction ratio is 2 : 1 so exact neutralisation **(1)**
	c)	Q = (240 + 75) x 4.18 x 5.2 = 6846.8 J **(1)** $\Delta H^{\ominus}_{neut1}$ = 6846.8 / 0.06 = 114,114 J mol^{-1} = **114 kJ mol^{-1}** **(1)**
	d)	Moles of NaOH = moles HCl = 0.500 x 25 / 1000 = 0.0125 mol **(1)** Equation is 1 : 1 Energy released = 57900 x 0.0125 = 723.75 J = Q **(1)** 723.75 = (25.0 + 25.0) x 4.18 x ΔT ΔT = 723.75 / (50.0 x 4.18) = **3.46 K or 3.46 °C rise (1)**
	e)	Ethanoic acid is a weak acid so the amount of $^{H+}$ ions in the solution is low. **(1)** The bond holding the acidic hydrogen in the carboxylic acid group onto the molecule needs breaking before neutralisaing. **(1)** The releasing of the H$^+$ is endothermic (bond breaking) which reduces the magnitude of the exothermic change for the neutralisation. **(1)**

Question 34	a)	$2\ HCl_{(aq)} + 2\ RbHCO_{3(s)} \rightarrow Rb_2CO_{3(s)} + CO_{2(g)} + H_2O_{(l)} + 2\ HCl_{(aq)}$ $2\ \Delta H_{R2} \qquad\qquad\qquad\qquad \Delta H_{R1}$ $\qquad 2\ RbCl_{(aq)}\ +\ 2\ CO_{2(g)}\ +\ 2\ H_2O_{(l)}$ *Reaction 1* Moles of Rb_2CO_3 = 4.62 / (2x85.5 + 60) = 0.0200 mol **(1)** Q = 100.0 x 4.18 x 2.2 = 919.6 J **(1)** ΔH_{R1} = 919.6 / 0.0200 = 45,980 J mol^{-1} = **− 46.0 kJ mol^{-1} to 3 s.f. (1)** (The 0.5 mol dm^{-3} is not a significant quantity as it is a chemical in excess.) *Reaction 2* Moles of $RbHCO_3$ = 4.40 / (85.5 + 1 + 60) = 0.0300 mol **(1)** Q = 100.0 x 4.18 x 2.3 = 961.4 J **(1)** ΔH_{R1} = 961.4 / 0.0300 = 32,047 J mol^{-1} = **+ 32.0 kJ mol^{-1} to 3 s.f. (1)** (The 0.5 mol dm^{-3} is not a significant quantity as it is a chemical in excess.) *Conversion Reaction* ΔH_R = 2 ΔH_{R2} − ΔH_{R1} = 2 x +32.0 + 46.0 **(1)** = **+ 110 kJ mol^{-1} to 3 s.f. (1)**
	b)	$RbHCO_3$ is more thermally stable than Rb_2CO_3. **(1)** The likely reaction is for Rb_2CO_3 to convert into $RbHCO_3$ over a period of time. **(1)**
Question 36	a)	$\Delta H_{Solution} = -\ \Delta H_{Lattice} + \Delta H_{Hydration}[Na^+_{(g)}] + \Delta H_{Hydration}[Br^-_{(g)}]$ $\Delta H_{Solution}$ = +742 − 405 − 348 **(1)** $\Delta H_{Solution}$ = **− 11.0 kJ mol^{-1} (1)**
	b)	Moles of NaBr = 14.7 / (23.0 + 79.9) = 0.1429 moles **(1)** Energy released (exothermic $\Delta H_{solution}$) = 0.1429 x 11 x 1000 = 1571.9 J **(1)** Q = m c ΔT so ΔT = 1571.9 / (250 x 4.18) = **1.5 °C rise (1)**

Question 37	a)	$Q = 255.0 \times 4.18 \times 0.86 = 916.674$ J **(1)** $\Delta H^{\ominus}_{solution} = 916.674 / 0.0550 = 16{,}666.8$ J mol^{-1} **(1)** $\Delta H^{\ominus}_{solution} = \mathbf{+\ 17}$ **kJ mol^{-1} to 2 s.f. (1)**
	b)	 Both gaseous ions correct **(1)** Both aqueous ions correct **(1)**
	c)	Sum of hydration energies $= \Delta H_{Lattice} + \Delta H^{\ominus}_{solution}$ $= -\,1755 + 17 = -\,1738$ kJ mol^{-1} $-\,1738 = 2 \times -\,524 + \Delta H_{Hydration}[M^{2+}]$ **(1)** $\Delta H_{Hydration}[M^{2+}] = -\,1738 + 1048$ **(1)** $= \mathbf{-\ 690}$ **kJ mol^{-1} to 2 s.f. (1)**
Question 37	a)	 Cycle correct **(1)** $\Delta H_{Lattice} = \Delta H_{hydr}[Sr^{2+}_{(g)}] + 2 \times \Delta H_{hydr}[I^{-}_{(g)}] + -\ \Delta H_{sol}[SrI_{2(s)}]$ $\Delta H_{Lattice} = -\,1443 + 2 \times -\,295 + +\,70$ **(1)** $\Delta H_{Lattice} = -\,1963$ kJ mol^{-1} **(1)**
	b)	Moles of SrI$_2$ dissolved $= 4.3 / (87.6 + 2 \times 126.9)$ $= 0.0126$ moles **(1)** Energy released from dissolving $= 0.0126 \times 70.0$ $= 0.882$ kJ $= 882$ J **(1)** Temperature change $= 882 / (4.18 \times 250) = \mathbf{0.84\ °C}$ **(1)** Temperature will rise as exothermic ΔH_{sol} **(1)**

Acknowledgements

I hope you have found this book to contain useful and thought-provoking practise in addition to your existing questions and that it has enhanced your understanding. No doubt there may be unintentional mistypes and errors so any feedback to mrevbooks@outlook.com will be very much appreciated along with any requests for future question topics.

There will soon be a website containing corrections to the mistakes as well as typographical and omission errors along with any further explanations at www.mrevbooks.co.uk.

This book came out of the preparation of materials for teaching A-level Chemistry and the lack of practice questions in published whole course textbooks.

The questions originated as a range of homework tasks and tests. I therefore have to thank all the students who studied GCE Chemistry at both Uplands Community College and Beacon Academy in East Sussex where many of the questions were trialled and tested along with the other schools where I have taught in recent years and created materials.

I am also developing a series of videos with follow-up questions and answers supporting A-level course content. Search for MrEV Chemistry on YouTube. Please subscribe!

The biggest thanks of all must go to my partner Hayley who uses her not inconsiderable proof-reading and language skills to rectify the typing errors and poorly worded questions on the first drafts of the content and encouraged me to create these books in the first place.

Thank you for buying and I wish you every success in your future endeavours, wherever they may lead you.

MrEV © 2020

Printed in Great Britain
by Amazon